# TREE LORE

# TREE LORE

## Magic, Myth, and Wisdom from Root to Bough

DAWN NELSON

Illustrated by Julia Asenbaum

**Countryman Press**

*An Imprint of W. W. Norton & Company*
*Independent Publishers Since 1923*

**Note to the Reader:** TREE LORE is a general interest book about the stories, lore, symbolism, and botanical features of trees. While the book discusses various ways in which parts of different trees may be used, the author is neither a nutritionist nor a physician, and TREE LORE is not, and should not be considered to be, a medical or nutritional text or guide. Please do not eat, drink, or otherwise use any part of any tree for nutritional or medicinal purposes without doing your own research with qualified professional sources to determine both whether you can do so safely, and what specific preparations, if any, you need to undertake before you can do so safely. If you are pregnant or nursing, or if you have any chronic medical condition such as but not limited to kidney disease or a bleeding disorder, consult your healthcare provider before you ingest or apply any tree-based substance.

Conceived, edited, and designed by Quarto Publishing, an imprint of The Quarto Group. Published by Countryman Press, an imprint of W. W. Norton & Company, Inc.

Copyright © 2026 by Quarto Publishing plc
Illustration copyright © 2026 by Julia Asenbaum

All rights reserved
Printed in Malaysia
First Edition

For information about permission to reproduce selections from this book, write to Permissions, Countryman Press, 500 Fifth Avenue, New York, NY 10110

For information about special discounts for bulk purchases, please contact W. W. Norton Special Sales at specialsales@wwnorton.com or 800-233-4830

Countryman Press
www.countrymanpress.com

An imprint of W. W. Norton & Company, Inc.
500 Fifth Avenue, New York, NY 10110
www.wwnorton.com

Authorized EU representative: EAS, Mustamäe tee 50, 10621 Tallinn, Estonia

978-1-324-11194-8

1 2 3 4 5 6 7 8 9 0

# CONTENTS

Introduction  6

### Chapter 1
### FIRE: TREES OF LIGHT
### 9

| | |
|---|---|
| Oak | 10 |
| Redwood | 14 |
| Birch | 18 |
| Pomegranate | 22 |
| Frankincense | 26 |
| Avocado | 30 |
| Joshua | 34 |

### Chapter 2
### WATER: TREES OF BEGINNING
### 39

| | |
|---|---|
| Baobab | 40 |
| Hazel | 44 |
| European Ash | 48 |
| Golden Wattle | 52 |
| Ceiba | 56 |
| Coco de Mer | 60 |
| Magic Guarri | 64 |

### Chapter 3
### AIR: TREES OF RESILIENCE
### 69

| | |
|---|---|
| Willow | 70 |
| Bay Laurel | 74 |
| Ginkgo | 78 |
| Sugar Maple | 82 |
| Wollemi Pine | 86 |
| Pipal | 90 |
| Rowan | 94 |

### Chapter 4
### EARTH: TREES OF LIFE
### 99

| | |
|---|---|
| Olive | 100 |
| Fig | 104 |
| Wild Apple | 108 |
| Yoshino Cherry | 112 |
| Koa | 116 |
| Cinchona | 120 |
| Kauri Pine | 124 |

### Chapter 5
### SPIRIT: TREES OF THE LIMINAL SPACE  129

| | |
|---|---|
| Date Palm | 130 |
| Elm | 134 |
| Palo Santo | 138 |
| Yew | 142 |
| Myrrh | 146 |
| Indian Banyan | 150 |
| Hawthorn | 154 |

| | |
|---|---|
| Index | 158 |
| Acknowledgments | 160 |

# INTRODUCTION

Welcome to the forest of *Tree Lore*, a place to rest, recuperate, and bathe in the dappled light filtering through the arboreous arms of the branches above. By walking this path through the trees, connecting with them and the landscape they inhabit, we will explore their stories, lore, and sacred symbolism. With the elements of Fire, Water, Air, Earth, and Spirit to guide us, we will reach out to touch their bark, examine their leaves, and embrace the gifts they offer us.

For thousands of years, humans have relied on trees for the resources that contribute to our success as a species—fuel, food, medicine, tools, weapons, transport, building material, and the very air we breathe. The significance of trees in our cultures is represented in place names, the words we use in our languages, and the roles they play in our faiths and religions. For example, the Old English word for tree, *trēow*, can also mean trust, faith, or promise—and the trees stand fast around us, reminding us of this truth.

In 2020, Botanic Gardens Conservation International (BGCI) spent two years researching and compiling a database of trees from across the world. They recorded 375,500 species of tree. This book holds thirty-five of those trees, and they have been chosen for their lore and stories. Given that this is less than 1 percent of the species recorded by the BGCI, there are many more tales for you to find in the woods, and this is by no means a definitive collection.

The trees have been grouped into five chapters to represent the elements of Fire, Water, Air, Earth, and Spirit. These five elements are the guiding structure for many nature-based faiths and are present in the world around us without us necessarily being consciously aware of them. Trees contain all five of these elements: Water from which they grow, Fire with which they are tempered, Air from which they pass us vital phytoncides and oxygen, the Earth

from which they are born, and the Spirit they hold within them. The trees in each chapter have been chosen according to the dominant corresponding element present in their lore, stories, and botany.

In writing this book, I have endeavored to research primary sources where Indigenous peoples are concerned and to respect the mythology, lore, faith, and stories held within these communities. Ultimately, we are all connected by our universal affinity for trees and the natural elements that lie within them, and there are similarities, too, within the cultures connecting us.

We once had swathes of wild woods across the world. With deforestation these wild places are now few and far between, and plantations and conurbations have replaced them, but with awareness of the climate crisis, many are finding ways to reconnect with the land and reforest areas that desperately need our help. For almost four hundred million years trees have lived on this planet; for six million years they have been silent partners in our ancestors' success. It's time for us to reconnect with these ancient beings and to learn from each other's cultures in order to nurture the forests of the future.

## HOW TO USE THIS BOOK

At the beginning of each chapter there is a short description of the element for that section and its connection with the stories, lore, and botanical features of those trees. The description for each tree indicates the magic it holds and how it may be used to help with everyday challenges, rituals, and intention setting. Each chapter holds seven trees, and their stories include anecdotes, folk tales, fables, lore, legend, and myth. The tales offer the reader new and old ways to look at trees and tap into the part of us that learns through story, reminding us of our connection with the natural world.

At the end of each of the featured trees, you will find an affirmation that invites you to pause and consider the tree's message. These affirmations can be used in a variety of ways; it's entirely up to you. Some suggestions include using the affirmations as an invitation to meditate on the message of that tree, or as a journaling prompt to help you explore the tree further, or even give you the motivation you need to take a walk and find that tree if it is present where you live. If it is not, the illustrations that accompany each tree will evoke a sense of that tree and allow you to do this remotely. The trees in this book offer a tool for personal meditation and spiritual practice within the home, as well as provide a connection with the landscapes of the world, their history, and heritage.

Chapter 1

# FIRE: TREES OF LIGHT

The human race owes much of its success to the element of Fire. In the forest, fire can be a destructive force, but it helps to control the understory, and from the ashes comes rebirth, light, courage, and passion. The forest knows that without fire it cannot thrive. In the desert, the light of the sun burns bright, yet forests thrive here, too, and at night the fire of the stars holds the stories of the trees. Associated with the energy of the "Red Planet," Mars, Fire is a masculine energy and also represents wrath and conflict, a theme we often find within the stories of our forests.

# OAK
*Quercus*

## *A tree of protection and strength that provides both food and shelter*

A familiar friend in the woods and forests of the Northern Hemisphere, there are around 450 oak species. They are long-lived trees and valued as both a human resource and a habitat that provides shelter for over two thousand species of insects, birds, and mammals.

Easily distinguished by the lobed, smooth-edged leaves, there are both evergreen and deciduous species within the *Quercus* genus. The oak is a pioneer tree, being one of the first plants to establish new territory in a woodland. Oaks develop distinctive corrugated, gnarled bark as they mature and the cascading yellow catkins turn into acorns, a nutlike fruit that sits in a small cup, from late summer until early winter. The acorns provide valuable food for pigs, cows, and sheep, and during the Middle Ages woodlands were valued according to how much livestock could be grazed there. The more acorns and beechnuts a woodland provided, the more it was worth. This practice is called pannage and continues to this day in the New Forest, England, and across the Iberian Peninsula, home to Dehesa, the largest open forest in Western Europe. As well as feeding livestock, acorns are also one of the oldest forms of food for humans. When dried and ground to a powder, they can be used to make a drink similar to coffee and to bulk out flour for bread making.

Oak galls, which form on the tree in late spring, are the work of the oak gall wasp (from the family Cynipidae). About the size of a marble, oak galls provide nests for this little wasp. In midsummer, when the young wasps have hatched, the galls can be harvested and used to make ferrous oak gall ink. This ink was used to write some of the earliest manuscripts, including the *Codex Sinaiticus*, the oldest and most complete version of the Bible in existence, which is over 1,600 years old.

## FIRE CORRESPONDENCE

Lightning • Protection • Justice

Fire lies at the heart of the oak tree and the gods with which it is associated. Thor from the Norse, Donar from the Saxon, Taranis from the Celtic, Zeus from the Greek, and Jupiter from the Roman pantheons are all weather gods with strong connections to thunder and lightning.

History tells us that in the eighth century an oak tree growing in northern Hesse, Germany, was for many years used as a community meeting place. Known as Donar's Oak, it was sacred to the Germanic pagans and had a close association with Thor, the Norse-Germanic god of justice. But during a time when the Christian church was discouraging alternative heathen religions, a man named Boniface was sent to cut down the tree. The oak was said to shriek and groan as it fell, and the community was sure Thor would strike Boniface down for his actions. However, this did not happen, which they took as a sign that they should convert to Christianity, and a church was built in place of Donar's Oak.

The oak is thought to be a place of shelter in a storm, but due to its long taproots and height compared to other forest trees, it is often struck by lightning, which means we find conflicting folklore surrounding the tree's association with lightning. If an oak is struck in a storm, it is considered a sacred tree touched by the hands of the gods. Consequently, people have been known to travel for miles to collect the ash and charred pieces of an oak tree struck by lightning. This close connection with lightning meant that ships were often built with oak because it was considered to be a charm against bad weather at sea. Most of the six hundred trees used to build Henry VIII's flagship, the *Mary Rose*, in the early sixteenth century were oak.

Oak trees have strong links to several kings, both real and legendary. Charles II was said to have hidden in an oak tree to avoid capture after the Battle

*If an oak is struck in a storm, it is considered a sacred tree touched by the hands of the gods.*

of Worcester in 1651, the last battle of the English Civil War, in which he was defeated by Oliver Cromwell's troops. When Charles was finally restored to the throne in 1660, the day was celebrated as Oak Apple Day on May 29. This is perhaps why the oak tree is associated with protection and strength, with couples in England marrying beneath an oak during this time. The oak tree has links to fabled kings, too, with King Arthur's Round Table purportedly made from oak, while the mythical Oak King appears in the guise of an oak tree each year for the summer and winter solstices.

The Oak King is said to hold the light of the sun during winter before releasing it into the world from the winter solstice to the summer solstice (around December 21 to June 21 in the Northern Hemisphere). The Holly King is his counterpart, taking the light back on the summer solstice and returning it to the Oak King at the winter solstice. The Oak King is often portrayed in the foliate faces found on pews, bench ends, and choir stalls of European churches: a reminder that he holds the light for us and will return again in summer.

> Look to the oak tree for stability in times of change.
>
> Affirmation

# REDWOOD
*Sequoioideae*

## *A gentle giant that represents peace and balance*

The tallest tree in the world is a coastal redwood (*Sequoia sempervirens*). It stands 379 feet (116 m) tall and around 16 feet (5 m) in diameter. While we know this tree is in the Redwood National Park, in California, its exact location is a secret. This tree has a name: Hyperion, after the Titan of Greek myth. With a name meaning "he who walks high," in the Greek pantheon, Hyperion is the father of Helios, the sun god, and a god of light in his own right. But this is not where the redwood's story begins.

The giant redwood (*Sequoiadendron giganteum*) is at least 145 million years old and native to Sierra Nevada, California. It can live up for to two thousand years, with one report citing a specimen that reached four thousand years. It is a coniferous tree, producing needles and self-pollinating cones, but the key to the redwood's success—in both height and age—lies in the tannin in its bark. The soft, fibrous, outer layer of the redwood's trunk can be up to 1 foot (30 cm) thick and contains high levels of tannins, making it resistant to disease and, most importantly, fire.

The redwood understands the importance of balance. Smaller wildfires help the tree, keeping the forest understory in check and encouraging new growth. In addition, the ash left behind by a fire creates an excellent fertilizer for these forest giants. It's when these fires get out of hand that disaster strikes, but even through this the redwood will persevere. If the redwood's trunk has been significantly damaged by a fire hot enough to pierce its bark, the tree can heal and regenerate, with new redwoods springing up from the old tree's roots. The new trees grow in a ring around the old one, taking advantage of the parent tree's root system. This ring is sometimes known as a fairy ring or family circle, the former nickname perhaps arriving with the Europeans.

## FIRE CORRESPONDENCE
Light • Healing • Purification

The redwood can take in water from the fog and snow prevalent in its habitat at various times of year, which in turn creates rain. It can store more carbon than any other tree, helping to purify the air we breathe and working against global warming.

Despite being endangered itself, it is also home to endangered animal species such as the marbled murrelet bird (*Brachyramphus marmoratus*), which lays its eggs in the redwood's branches, and the Coho salmon (*Oncorhynchus kisutch*), which lays eggs in the roots of the trees that grow on the banks of Redwood Creek, Humboldt County. Redwoods live in a community, stabilizing each other with their roots, and it is believed only a lightning strike will stop them from growing.

To the Indigenous peoples of the region, the redwood is a sacred tree and to fell it an act of violence. If timber is needed, only fallen trees are used. The Yurok and Tolowa peoples relied on fire to hollow out the trunks of fallen trees to make canoes, while the Miwok and Pomo used the leaves in a poultice to cure earache. The cones can stay on the trees, high up in the canopy, for up to twenty years. We do not know what triggers the cones to fall, although Indigenous women will tell you that singing to the trees will make this

*In Miwok creation stories, animals and plants were once people, and the redwoods were, and still are, the village elders.*

happen. The redwood is a peaceful tree that tells a story of balance, showing the past and the future in the present.

The redwood gained worldwide fame during the California Gold Rush of the nineteenth century when Europeans arrived in the area. With them they brought a zeal for commercialization. In one case dating to 1853, a giant sequoia tree that had stood on Miwok land for hundreds of years was felled by Gold Rush speculators. A section of the trunk was hollowed out and taken to San Francisco. The floor inside the trunk was carpeted and a piano and seating installed inside so people could pay to sit in the "tree salon." Even in the cultural climate of the 1800s, people were aware that these ancient beings should not be treated in such a way, and many called for the redwoods to be preserved, denouncing their destruction as vandalism.

As the centuries rolled by, logging progressed and heavy machinery took the place of hand tools, making the felling of a tree possible within hours rather than the weeks it once took to cut down one of these giants. Consequently, of the two million acres (810,000 ha) of coastal redwood that once existed, only 5 percent remains. The coastal redwood —along with the giant redwood—is now considered endangered.

For the Miwok people, the redwood remains a sacred tree. In their creation stories, animals and plants were once people, and the redwoods were, and still are, the village elders. It is said that the red bark of these trees reminds us of the blood that flows in all our veins. Conservationists are today striving to protect the community of giant redwoods still growing in Sierra Nevada.

In Kings Canyon National Park, in the southern Sierra Nevada, stands a giant redwood known as the General Grant Tree. This became the "Nation's Christmas Tree" in 1926 after a young girl stood at its base, looked up, and wondered how many lights it would take to turn this mighty being into a Christmas tree. Now, each year, locals visit the tree to sing carols and pray, allowing the redwood to take its place at the heart of a human community once more.

> ## Look to the redwood as a beacon in the forest.
>
> ---
>
> Affirmation

# BIRCH
*Betula*

## *A pioneer species signifying abundance and fertility*

The birch was one of the first trees to establish itself in Europe after the Ice Age over two million years ago. Our Neolithic ancestors would chew birch tar to treat gum inflammation. Thriving on dry soil, birch can be found on heathland, which was once, and often still is, common land that provided green public spaces as well as a home to rare species of invertebrates, reptiles, and amphibians. As a pioneer species, birch can easily colonize these flat, open expanses. However, balance must be restored if there is abundant birch in order to preserve that very habitat.

Birch trees have distinctive, silvery white, papery bark, resulting in three species names: silver birch (*Betula pendula*), paper birch (*Betula papyrifera*), and downy birch (*Betula pubescens*). The birch is shorter than many of its arboreal cousins, with delicate, translucent, triangular leaves. The tree bears both male and female catkins, allowing for self-pollination. Once pollinated, the female catkins turn deep red, while in the fall the leaves become a fiery gold.

The birch is associated with the Irish god Lugh, god of light and the sun, and wielder of a fiery sword. Lugh is a member of the Tuatha Dé Danann, a race of ethereal people with magical powers, thought by some to be the original inhabitants of Ireland. It is said that the god Ogma was born with the ability to write and created the Ogham alphabet, a series of runic marks, with each representing a different tree. He developed this skill to warn Lugh that the Sidhe, a race of Irish fairies, were planning to kidnap his wife, Buí. Surrounding her with birch was the only way to protect her—birch is now the first letter of the Ogham alphabet.

Birch speaks of abundance, birth, and fertility. On May Day (May 1), red and white ribbons are tied to the cut

# FIRE CORRESPONDENCE

Sun • Sexuality • Pioneers

branches of young birch trees and placed at the doors of stables, barns, and houses to ward off malevolent spirits, witches, and fae folk known to walk on the eve of May Day (April 30). The branches are then left in place all year.

May Day celebrations such as Beltane, maypole dancing, and feasting are thought to be associated with fertility rituals, both ancient and modern. Beltane is a relatively modern festival in the neo-pagan Wheel of the Year but is based on very old practices involving balefires and blessing cattle before they return to their summer pastures. On the eve of May Day, it is thought couples would go courting in the birch woods. The ribboned poles known as maypoles, around which people dance, were also often made of birch. Although sometimes purpose-cut, a rooted tree might also be used. The tradition of ribbon dancing can be found in the UK, Spain, Scandinavia, and Latin America.

The belief that birch could drive out evil spirits led local communities to walk the parish boundary, beating the ground with birch sticks. Bundles of birch are also used to sweep out the old and usher in the new. Indeed, birch branches make excellent besom brooms. These are strongly associated with witches, so much so that the growths seen on birch branches, which look like upside-down brooms (caused by a fungus called *Taphrina betulina*), are known as witches' brooms. "Archie's Besom," a story originating in Argyll, Scotland, tells the tale of how these brooms ended up in birch trees.

*According to Slavic folklore, the birch tree not only holds life but also the souls of the deceased, making it a tree of regeneration.*

In Scotland and Wales, jumping the broom is traditionally observed on a wedding night, with the husband required to leap over the broom first on entering the new couple's home. If any woman, not just his wife, stepped over the broom first, they would immediately fall pregnant. In the Fourth Branch of the *Mabinogi*, an eleventh-century Welsh text, the goddess Arianrhod is tested to see if she is a maiden in order to become King Math's foot-holder. As she jumps over a branch that Math has placed on the ground, she gives birth to two children, one of whom is Lleu Llaw Gyffes, the Welsh equivalent of the Irish Lugh. The story does not say whether the branch is birch, but the similarity in the folklore is striking.

Later, the tradition of jumping the broom traveled from the Celtic world to America, becoming an important part of African American culture. The tradition there may have evolved at a time when enslaved people were denied the right to marry—jumping the broom was used symbolically to show that a couple were beginning their lives together. However, another version of this story states that it was the enslavers who enforced this tradition.

An English colloquial name for the birch tree is "Lady of the Woods." Similarly, it is known as "Lady of the Forest" in the Slavic tradition. In many Slavic countries, a ceremony takes place in early summer on the seventh Thursday after Easter. This calls for specific rituals, including cleaning the home, hanging birch branches on doorways, bathing, steaming, and feasting. During this time, all work is prohibited, weddings take place, and funeral rites are held for those who have died young. According to Slavic folklore, the birch tree not only holds life but also the souls of the deceased, making it a tree of regeneration.

> **Turn to the birch tree to sweep out the old and make way for the new.**
>
> Affirmation

# POMEGRANATE
*Punica granatum*

## *The "Fruit of Paradise" is associated with renewed life*

The pomegranate, synonymous with luxury and fine dining, is native to southeastern Europe and southern Asia. Pomegranates have adorned our dinner tables since at least 5000 BCE, with the biggest exporters of this pretty, bright red berry being India and China. The fruit is rich in antioxidants and vitamins, making it a fashionable superfood. It is thought to soothe digestive complaints, support circulation, and even prevent some cancers, although the evidence for this is minimal. All these factors have gained the pomegranate the nickname "the Fruit of Paradise."

The pomegranate tree protects its harvest amid spiny branches. Delicate, trumpet-shaped red flowers turn into the round, red fruit we are more familiar with. A leathery, ruby-blush skin hides individual seeds nestled in a soft, white pith. The ancient Roman name for the pomegranate, *Malam granatum*, reflects the bounty of the seeds it holds. *Malam* translates as "apple" and *granatum* as "grain" or "seedlike." In Jewish lore, it is said that the pomegranate holds 613 seeds, correlating with the number of laws in the Old Testament.

The pomegranate's connection with religion is also seen in another of its colloquial names, "The Fruit of Paradise." Indeed, it is a sacred fruit in several faiths, including the ancient Zoroastrian religion, in which it symbolizes the sun and light. In Israel, the flowering of the pomegranate heralds spring and is connected to the Bible story of Moses leading the Israelites out of Egypt to freedom. Moses sends scouts to confirm that they have reached the Promised Land, and they come back with pomegranates, among other fruits.

In this way, the fruits have become associated with God's blessing in the Jewish faith, and alternating gold bells and pomegranates made of red and

## FIRE CORRESPONDENCE

Summer • Power • Desires

blue wool once adorned the hem of the high priest's robes. Pomegranates also decorated the pillars of King Solomon's Temple in Jerusalem, which was destroyed around 600 BCE. Today, during the Jewish New Year, Rosh Hashanah, pomegranates are eaten to break the fast, and a blessing is recited to thank God for the gift of this fruit.

Several ancient Greek myths feature the pomegranate. The plant is said to have grown from the blood of Dionysus when he found himself on the receiving end of the goddess Hera's wrath. Semele, a human seduced by Zeus, was the mother of Dionysus. When Hera discovered this affair, one of many conducted by Zeus, she sliced Dionysus into many pieces and boiled him in a pot. From his blood grew the pomegranate tree. Dionysus' grandmother, the Titan Rhea, brought him back to life, and he became known as the god of fruitfulness, plenty, revelry, and wine.

In the Greek myth of Hades and Persephone, the pomegranate is associated with the returning of the light. This is not a romantic myth and has violence at its heart. Persephone's story is one of the most famous Greek myths and is still told to this day.

Hades, Persephone's uncle, abducts his niece against her will to live as his wife in the Underworld. When the grief and rage of Demeter, Persephone's mother, stop the harvests of the world and threaten to damage the reputation of the gods, Zeus insists that Hades return Persephone, as long as she has not eaten any food in the Underworld. Persephone has not, but Hades tricks her into eating six pomegranate seeds before she returns to the surface. This trickery means that Persephone can only spend six months aboveground each year with Demeter and must return to Hades for the remaining six.

It is from this story that we have the origins of summer and winter: summer

*In the Greek myth of Hades and Persephone, the pomegranate is associated with the returning of the light.*

being the glorious months of plenty when Persephone and Demeter are reunited, and winter the dark months in which they are separated once more.

The Granada Mollar de Elche pomegranate is thought to have been grown in Elche, Spain, since the third century CE. For this reason it has a Protected Designation of Origin. Spain has a long history of growing pomegranates and, as a result, you will find the pomegranate in many historic Tudor buildings in the south of England. This is because Catherine of Aragon, Henry VIII's first wife, took the pomegranate as her symbol and as a reminder of her Spanish homeland. Catherine followed the Catholic faith, in which the pomegranate appears as a religious symbol associated with motherhood, the Virgin Mary, and the Passion of Christ.

Often carved into the Tudor royal household's furniture and buildings, the pomegranate appears side by side with Henry Tudor's rose, representing the union of England and Spain. Furthermore, the sister ship to Henry's *Mary Rose* was called the *Peter Pomegranate* in honor of Catherine of Aragon. Their marriage lasted twenty-four years until she was divorced by Henry and ousted as queen by Anne Boleyn. Yet the pomegranate has remained carved on buildings, furnishings, and belongings associated with Henry VIII for far longer than the duration of the House of Tudor.

# Look to the pomegranate for light in the darkness.

Affirmation

# FRANKINCENSE
*Boswellia*

*Promotes peace, clarity, and connection with the divine*

Frankincense trees grow in the wadis, the long, arid, sweeping valleys of Arabia, which often only have water in winter. A relatively small tree, the frankincense tree has the palest of yellow flowers and a paper-thin bark that is easily removed. With a bifurcating trunk and buttress root system anchoring the tree in the ground, frankincense is adept at growing in places many trees would find hostile.

The frankincense tree is known as *al-lubān* in Arabic and is a member of the torchwood family (Burseraceae), so-called because the high resin content of the branches makes them easily flammable and therefore excellent for use as torches. The tree starts producing resin at around eight years old. The resin will start oozing out in small droplets if the bark is peeled from the trunk. Depending on the species, the resin can vary in color from white to amber-gold. Highly prized for its scent, the resin releases an aroma of wood, smoke, lemon, and spices when heated and burned. The word "frankincense" is thought to come from the French words *franc* and *encens*, meaning "pure lighting."

For almost two thousand years, incense reached the West via the Incense Route. This was a series of trading routes connecting the Levant, Egypt, and northeastern Africa with the Mediterranean and Europe. However, by the third century CE, trade had decreased, perhaps due to the fall of the Roman Empire, which was a major player in these trade routes. Despite the decline during this period, frankincense continues to be one of the most popular perfume scents in the world.

Oman is famous for its frankincense, and the resin from the trees growing in the Dhofar Mountains is known as Hojari. Hojari is thought to be the finest frankincense in the world. Here, the

## FIRE CORRESPONDENCE
Phoenix • Torches • Divination

resin is burned in a double-handled clay brazier called a magmar. The burner's hourglass-shaped cup has an ornate, perforated design, which allows the scented smoke to be released.

Frankincense was used in ancient Egypt to invoke the god Anubis and open the Third Eye in a ritual called the Ink-pool, a form of scrying. Scrying is a method of divination that involves gazing into a black mirrored surface to divine images and messages from other worlds. In doing this, you could ask the god of the Underworld any questions you might have.

Many centuries later, the Anglo-Saxons used frankincense in their folk magic. A ritual using lupin, garlic, betony (*Betonica officinalis*), frankincense, and a fawn's skin was used to rid a man of nightmares. During the late medieval period in Poland, we see frankincense being used to remove bewitchments cast over beer and horses, while more contemporary uses of frankincense include clearing negative energy, cleansing spaces, and regulating emotions.

In the Bible, frankincense's association with royalty is sealed when

*Frankincense was used in ancient Egypt to invoke the god Anubis and open the Third Eye in a ritual called the Ink-pool.*

it becomes a gift from one of the three wise men. When Christ is thought to have been born, frankincense was more valuable than gold and indicated aristocracy and kinship. In this way, Mary and her carpenter husband, Joseph, received a form of approval through these gifts, initiating them into the aristocracy and indicating the role their son, Jesus, would play in the near future.

As you might expect, although frankincense may play a subsidiary role in stories, it always has significance and symbolism. For example, its value as a perfume is revealed in Shakespeare's *Macbeth* when Lady Macbeth declares: "All the perfumes of Arabia will not sweeten this little hand." In this guilt-induced sleepwalking scene, she is thought to be referring to scents such as frankincense, then favored by royalty.

In the Roman poet Ovid's *Metamorphoses,* frankincense is associated with the fire bird known as a phoenix. Ovid describes how the phoenix eats small drops of frankincense and strews its nest with frankincense, myrrh, cinnamon, cassia bark, and sweet spikenard. After five hundred years, the phoenix lies down to rest in the nest, then bursts into flames and arises anew from the ashes. This is echoed in the work of another Roman writer, Pliny the Elder, who describes the bird having purple feathers on its body, an azure-blue tail, and a ruff of golden plumage. Pliny also notes that the bird lines its nest with frankincense as well as other luxurious items.

A folk tale told in Oman, Yemen, and the Horn of Africa involves a young jinn girl who falls in love with a human. As magical beings far above the world of humans, the other jinn do not approve of her chosen partner and demand she be punished for her transgression. The young girl begs for her life, crying many tears, but the jinn do not relent and she must decide how she will be punished. She chooses to become a tree, and the jinn turn her into the frankincense tree. Through long days she now stands in the arid desert landscape, crying for her lost love, and the resin that springs from the peeled bark of the frankincense tree is said to be her tears.

## Look to frankincense for transformation.

---

Affirmation

# AVOCADO
*Persea americana*

## *A fruit of fertility in ancient folklore*

The avocado is native to a region between Mexico and Costa Rica, and was first grown in Mesoamerica. Avocado was a valued part of the diet of the Mexica people (the Aztecs who lived in present-day Mexico), enjoyed for its taste and revered as a sacred fruit. In addition to evidence that avocados were present in the Mesoamerican diet from around 10,000 BCE, archaeological investigations have also revealed an avocado-shaped water jar, dating from about 900 CE, which was found near the pre-Columbian city of Chan Chan (in present-day Peru).

The avocado is, in fact, a berry with a single large stone, and it grows naturally in the highlands between Mexico and Guatemala. Avocados are prized for their oil and health benefits because they contain high-density lipoprotein (HDL) cholesterol, or "good cholesterol," which is thought to lower the risk of heart disease.

The tree itself is relatively short, with dark green, oval leaves. The fruit takes at least three months to grow and ripens from clusters made up of tiny, six-petaled, lime-green flowers, which resemble inverted umbrellas. Avocado is a climacteric fruit, meaning it can ripen without being attached to the parent tree—a huge advantage when exporting the fruit over large distances. The fruit of different avocado varieties ranges in texture, size, shape, and color, from smooth- to rough-skinned, spherical to pear-shaped, and green to almost black.

The fruit's popularity has seen consumption in the UK rise from 18 ounces (0.5 kg) per person in 1989 to over 106 ounces (3 kg) in 2016. The trend is echoed across the Western world, and this popularity has put a strain on local infrastructures where avocados are grown, resulting in deforestation, a rise in organized crime, and depleted water supplies.

## FIRE CORRESPONDENCE
Passion • The Stars • Ambition

Avocados were not always so fashionable, only emerging as a middle-class staple after various campaigns promoting their virtues. The avocado was promoted in *Vogue* magazine in the late 1800s by the California Avocado Society as an upmarket addition to salad. A century later, in the 1990s, Californian avocado farmers hit upon the idea of promoting guacamole at the Super Bowl: the perfect accompaniment to the thousands of potato chips consumed at each game.

> *[The avocado] was prized by the Mesoamericans for its connection with fertility.*

The fruit's popularity has led to urban folklore in the form of news stories from the 2010s and 2020s, which blamed the avocado for an increase in knife injuries. These were a result of consumers holding the avocado in the palm of their hand as they jabbed the stone with the end of a knife in order to spear and remove it. In doing so, the knife often slipped off the stone and sliced through their palm. There is some truth in this myth, as shown by statistics in *The American Journal of Emergency Medicine* (Volume 38, Issue 5, May 2020). The article, "Avocado-Related Knife Injuries: Describing an Epidemic of Hand Injury," written by Kevin X. Farley et al., states that between 1998 and 2017, avocado hand injuries increased by about nine times, from around 3,000 from 1998 to 2002 to over 27,000 from 2013 to 2017.

The oils in avocado are said to be good for your cholesterol levels, skin, and hair, but the fruit was also prized by the Mesoamericans because of its connection with fertility. This is perhaps because of the fruit's shape and the way it hangs from the tree. In the language of the ancient Mexica people, the fruit was known as *āhuacatl,* meaning "testicle."

Ancient lore concerning the avocado among the Mexica people tells of a man named Seriokai. Seriokai loved avocados and would pick them all day, bringing them home to his wife. One day, a tapir entered the house while he was picking avocados. The tapir seduced his wife, and she fell madly in love with the creature. They planned to run away together, but first found Seriokai, who was, as usual, picking avocados. They hit him over the head, left him for dead, and stole his basket of avocados. Nursed back to health by a neighbor, Seriokai was soon on the trail of his wife and the tapir. He followed the avocado saplings that grew from the stones of the fruit they had eaten and discarded, and soon caught up with them. They ran to the ends of the Earth, with Seriokai following, and as they reached the edge of the Earth, Seriokai drew back his bow and fired an arrow into the sky. It arced high and found its place in the eye of the tapir, killing it and knocking it off the edge of the Earth. His wife, bereft, threw herself into the abyss after the tapir. Seriokai was so angry that he, too, followed them over the edge. It is said that the three of them are now forever in the sky, Seriokai as the constellation known in the West as Orion the Hunter, chasing Hyades (the tapir) and the Pleiades (Seriokai's wife). The passion that lived in their hearts is now in the fire of the stars.

## Look to the avocado for passion in your life.

---

Affirmation

# JOSHUA
*Yucca brevifolia*

## *An ancient and unpredictable tree of remarkable resilience*

The Joshua tree, a species of yucca dating back to before the Ice Age, is a highly specialized plant that mainly grows in the Mojave and Colorado Deserts in southern California, within Joshua Tree National Park. The Joshua prefers elevations of 1,300–6,600 feet (400–2,000 m) in places with little water and where the temperature is cooler, having adapted to survive in this hostile landscape. Joshua trees grow as solitary specimens or in forests, with tourists traveling from across the world to see these incredible trees.

The Joshua tree blooms, and therefore fruits, unpredictably. It bears light green, oval fruits with flat seeds, with productivity relying on the amount of rainfall in the area for that season. Joshuas are most likely to germinate during El Niño years—years when there is enough rainfall to allow their roots to establish—and for the first few years of their lives, they look very similar to a tuft of grass. If they survive the droughts, they will become overstory for creosote bush (*Larrea tridentata*) and pinyon-juniper, a desert scrub consisting of California juniper (*Juniperus californica*) and pinyon pine (*Pinus monophylla*). The tree's peculiar shape, coupled with the area's distinctive rock formations, make the home of this tree appear otherworldly.

The Joshua tree's spiky trunk and knife-shaped leaves hide pyramidal clusters of white flowers, which have an unusual smell and are at the center of a symbiotic relationship between the tree and the pronuba moth (*Tegeticula* species). The moth pollinates the tree and then lays its eggs in the flowers. The tree regulates this relationship by dropping flowers in which too many eggs have been laid.

As you would expect from such an ancient tree, it has had many names. To the Cahuilla, one of the groups

# FIRE CORRESPONDENCE
## Deserts • Faith • Blessings

of Indigenous people living in this area, it is known as *hunuvat chiy'a* or *humwichawa* and was once a valuable food source as well as useful for making rope, beds, sandals, and baskets. The roots can also be peeled and mashed together to make soap.

The oldest culture thought to have lived around the Colorado River, and in what is now Joshua Tree National Park, is the Pinto culture, from between 8000 and 4000 BCE. Then came the Maara'yam (Serrano), the Kawiya (Cahuilla), the Nüwü (Chemehuevi), and the Aha Macav (Mojave). Small numbers of these four Indigenous groups still live in the area and are recognized as the original stewards of this landscape.

The flower buds are the main edible part of the Joshua tree and are good to eat in mid-spring, as long as they are cooked. They can be roasted or boiled, with archaeological evidence in the form of roasting pits suggesting they have been a seasonal food for thousands of years. The roasting pits are difficult to date, as there are no artifacts in or around them, but evidence indicates they were used year after year and that the sites were only occupied for a few weeks, making the tree a highly seasonal food.

When colonists explored this area, the Joshua tree did not meet with a receptive audience. In 1844, John C. Fremont, of the US Army, detailed in a report describing an expedition through the Rocky Mountains, Oregon, and northern California that it was the "most repulsive tree in the vegetable kingdom." Joseph Smeaton Chase echoed this sentiment in his 1919 book *California Desert Trails*, describing the tree as "a misshapen pirate with belt boots hands and teeth stuck full of daggers." But the tree found sanctuary when the area was designated a national monument in 1936 by Franklin D. Roosevelt before finally becoming a national park in 1994.

*Urban lore associates the Joshua tree with the Skinwalkers, or* Yee Naaldlooshii.

Urban lore associates the Joshua tree with the Skinwalkers, or *Yee Naaldlooshii,* which are a part of the Navajo (Diné) people's stories. Skinwalkers are malevolent, shape-shifting beings able to disguise themselves as any animal. Many tourists who have walked among the trees at night report a feeling of being watched or followed.

A story connected to Mormon settlers reveals how the Joshua tree came by its English name. When the settlers were crossing the Mojave Desert in the mid-1800s, it is said the tree acted as a guide—a reminder of the Bible story in which Moses raises his hands to heaven to demonstrate his faith in God and that the Israelites, led by Joshua, would win the war against the Amalekites (enemies of the Israelites).

Climate change has seen the home of the Joshua tree become more and more uninhabitable, even for this resilient tree. Joshua Tree National Park has seen a 40 percent reduction in rainfall and a temperature increase of 3.6°F (2°C). These environmental changes, plus a proliferation of grasses, have in turn caused an increase in wildfires. Not only has this led to a decline in the number of Joshua trees but also in the many species of birds, reptiles, mammals, and insects that rely on this curious tree. By the end of the twenty-first century, the predicted rise in temperature could result in the tree's extinction. There is hope, however, that a species with us since at least the Ice Age will find a way to survive.

# Turn to the Joshua tree to draw on your inner strength.

Affirmation

Chapter 2

# WATER: TREES OF BEGINNING

The Water element is ever present in stories of creation. From great rivers, wells, and lakes come forth life. Once water is established, we find that these places of beginning become the homes of trees. As the water nourishes their roots, it is often from these trees of myth that humankind is born. And so it is that trees of Water represent fertility, abundance, feminine power, immortality, and the moon, with its influence on the ebb and flow of our tides. Among the trees of Water, we find stories of elves, wells, rivers, oceans, fishing boats, and more.

# BAOBAB
*Adansonia digitata*

## *A welcoming tree that encompasses both life and death*

An iconic tree native to the African continent, the baobab is also known as the upside-down tree, elephant tree, and Tree of Life. It can stand over 60 feet (18 m) tall and grow 30 feet (9 m) wide, with branches that stretch toward the sky. This gives the impression that the tree is upside down, an effect enhanced by the fact that its branches are bare for most of the year. When the baobab flowers, its quirky blooms are made of papery, white petals around a pom-pom of stamens.

Thought to be the oldest living species in Africa and possibly the world, the baobab tree can live for up to three thousand years, overcoming the arid conditions of its natural habitat, the savanna. A keystone species, it is fundamental to the ecosystems in which it thrives, providing food, shelter, and water for a multitude of insects and animals, as well as reducing soil erosion and retaining moisture in the earth.

The largest succulent in the world, the baobab is expert at water storage, drawing up thousands of gallons of water from deep underground and storing it in its vast trunk. The baobab reacts cautiously to change and adapts gradually to shifts in its environment, making it the ultimate slow liver. Baobabs are solitary trees, avoiding the competition in large forests and standing tall and alone, determined in their efforts to bring forth life.

To the African Bushmen, the baobab is a gateway to the spirit world. Burial rites were once performed within the hollowed-out trunks of old trees for significant members of the community, such as griots, who are the knowledge holders of the tribes. According to the Baobab Foundation, in some places it is believed that people who live beneath the baobab are likely to have more children, as a soup made from the leaves is rich in vitamin C, increasing the

## WATER CORRESPONDENCE
Patience • Reservoirs • Birth

fertility of women who consume it and helping to keep young children healthy. In this way, the baobab tree is connected to both life and death.

> *It is said that the creator god threw the tree out of his garden when he decided it had no place in his paradise.*

Many stories relate how the baobab tree came to be. Most involve someone losing their temper with the baobab, whether through the tree's own doing or for no other reason than the way it looks. It is said that the creator god threw the tree out of his garden when he decided it had no place in his paradise. The tree flew over the wall and landed upside down, but continued to thrive.

In another African creation story, Hyena is responsible for the baobab's topsy-turvy look when she is late to a gathering in which the creator asks the animals to plant a tree. She ends up with a peculiar-looking sapling and, disgusted with what she has been given, throws it away. The sapling roots itself upside down, and the rest is history.

In other stories the tree talks itself into its predicament, complaining to the creator multiple times as it grows about its lack of height, flowers, and fruit, and rejecting all the creator's gifts. Eventually, the creator loses patience with the tree and uproots it, but not wishing to end its life, he thrusts it in the ground the wrong way up.

The origin of the baobab tree's height, and perhaps a nod to its ability to store water, appears in another story involving Hyena. In this tale, Hyena steals into a house where she eats a pot of grease as well as the young girl stirring it. In retaliation, the girl's sister drains the water hole and takes the water to the top of a baobab tree. As the animals pass below, she offers them water in exchange for coughing up her sister. Each time she asks and her sister is not returned, the baobab grows taller until eventually Hyena passes by and the younger sister is returned.

While generally a welcoming and protective tree associated with fertility and health, the baobab also has a dark side. Pick one of those beautiful, white blossoms, and lore has it that you will find yourself being consumed by a lion. The baobab is also a jealous tree, as a tale about a baobab in Kafue National Park, in Zambia, shows. Known as *Kondanamwali*, which means "tree that eats maidens," the story goes that the tree fell in love with four young girls living beneath it. When they came of age and married, the tree grew so jealous it opened its leathery, gray trunk and swallowed them up.

Where there are baobab groves, you will often find settlements. In its welcoming branches, bees produce honey, animals seek shelter, and humans glean fibers for rope, remedies for fevers, protein and oil from the fruits, and vital vitamins from the leaves. The baobab is truly the Tree of Life. Even when elephants strip its bark in search of water, this tree has learned to overcome wounds that would fell others. Through millennia, the baobab shrinks and swells, adapting to a dearth or a plethora of water and giving back much more than it takes.

# Look to the baobab tree for abundance.

Affirmation

# HAZEL
*Corylus*

## *A versatile tree with many practical and mystical uses*

The common hazel (*Corylus avellana*) is native to Europe and western Asia. Although a short-lived deciduous tree, living no more than eighty years, coppicing by humans can extend its lifespan for hundreds of years.

The ancient craft of coppicing has been carried out in woodlands across the world for centuries. Hazel is coppiced in an eight-year cycle, with the branches cut at the base, creating a stool from which new branches will grow. Hazel stools can reach 6½ feet (2 m) across, and the coppiced branches can be used for firewood, wattle for fencing and walls, thatching spars, and fishing rods.

The American hazel (*Corylus americana*) is an important resource for Indigenous peoples and is used for basket making, food, medicine, and sometimes ceremonial drumsticks. Hazel is still coppiced in many places as a conservation technique to create habitats for plants and wildlife, and to extend the life of a tree.

A member of the Betulaceae family, hazel resembles the silver birch tree (*Betula pendula*), with spade-like leaves in spring, although these are much larger than those of the birch and heart-shaped at the base. The hazel's smooth bark provides an important home for lichens, liverworts, and mosses, the keystone species of many habitats. The fallen branches also offer sanctuary to the scarlet elfcup fungus (*Sarcoscypha austriaca*), so-called because its fruiting body resembles a small, dew-collecting cup that might be used by forest elves. The hazel is often the first tree in woods and hedgerows to produce its pendulous, bright yellow catkins, which appear in late December and early January in the Northern Hemisphere.

The fruit of the hazel is a brown nut that ripens in the fall. A vital food source for many woodland residents,

## WATER CORRESPONDENCE
Renewal • Wisdom • Transformation

it is thought hunter-gatherers in the Mesolithic Period—around 9,000 to 4,300 years ago—also ate hazelnuts. As an itinerant population, they often carried the nuts with them, spreading the hazel across continents. Others suggest the hazelnut was introduced and cultivated by the ancient Greeks and Romans in much of Europe.

The word hazelnut comes from the Old English *haesel knut*, meaning "cap nut," a nod to the little cap of leaves in which the nut sits. In medieval England the nuts were used as charms against rheumatism, while in China, nuts from the Chinese hazel (*Corylus chinensis*) are thought to be good for the stomach and spleen, purifying the blood. Dioscorides, a Greek physician and botanist from the first century CE, recommended hazelnuts as a cure for colds and to encourage hair growth.

In England, until the beginning of the twentieth century, children would be given the day off school or work on Holy Cross Day (September 18) to go nutting. However, if the day fell on a Sunday and a girl went nutting, she would likely meet the devil and become pregnant out of wedlock. The collected nuts were often stored until Nut Crack Night, which took place around Halloween, when they were used to divine who young village girls might marry: names of suitors would be written on the nuts and thrown into a fire to see which one popped the loudest.

*In Greek mythology, Circe's wand, with which she turns all male visitors to her island into pigs, is said to be made from the magical hazel tree.*

The hazel is sacred in Celtic traditions, particularly those of Ireland and Scotland, and appears in the stories of the Fenian/Fianna Cycle. One story describes a salmon eating hazelnuts after they fell from nine hazel trees into the Well of Wisdom in the Otherworld. The number of spots on the salmon indicates how many hazelnuts it has eaten—the greater the number, the more wisdom the salmon holds. Eating this salmon will imbue you with poetic and prophetic wisdom and power.

In another story a warrior called Fionn goes on a journey to seek knowledge and encounters Finegas, a Druid who has spent seven years searching for the Salmon of Wisdom. During Fionn's apprenticeship, Finegas catches the salmon and places it on a skillet to cook. He leaves Fionn to cook the salmon, with strict instructions not to eat any of it. As the salmon cooks, hot fat hits Fionn's thumb. On putting his thumb in his mouth to cool it, he receives all the knowledge held by the salmon and meant for Finegas. From that point on, all Fionn must do to gain wisdom and insight is place his thumb in his mouth.

It is not only the nuts of the hazel that are sacred in lore. In Greek mythology, Circe's wand, with which she turns all male visitors to her island into pigs, is said to be made from the magical hazel tree, while a hazel staff is given to Hermes by Apollo as a tool to assist him on his travels between Olympia and Earth. Many centuries later, in Britain, hazel branches were used as staffs by Druids, prized for self-defense by those traveling the old roads, and shaped into shepherds' crooks. Hazel is also believed to offer protection from witches and fae folk. A fork of hazel can be used to dowse for water, and in some parts of England it was once used to find precious metals for mining. If you wish to use hazel as a magical tool, you must cut the branch after May Day, not before.

# Look to the hazel tree for wisdom.

Affirmation

# EUROPEAN ASH
*Fraxinus excelsior*

## *A magical tree representing stability and connection*

Found across the globe, even in the Arctic Circle, ash trees can live for hundreds of years—a coppiced ash stool in Bradfield Woods in Suffolk, England, may be over a thousand years old. Ash trees can reach 115 feet (35 m) and have graying bark that develops small cracks with age, giving the bark a rough texture. In late winter, the smooth twigs carry distinctive black leaf buds, and in spring each leaf cluster has up to six pairs of pinnate leaves. The summer fruits are known as keys because the seeds that hang from the branches resemble jailers' keys.

The ash lies at the heart of much Celtic lore. In Scotland, the ash is a magical tree whose roots extend deep underground, representing stability and resilience. In Ireland, lore tells of a wise man named Fintan who planted five trees, one in each corner of the country and the last in the middle. These trees were regarded as sacred, with ash comprising three of the five trees: *Bile Tortan* (The Tree of Magh Tortan), *Bile Uisneg* (The Branching Tree of Uisneach), and *Craebh Daithí* (The Sacred Tree of Creevna). In the nineteeth century, the English writer Robert Graves recorded a living descendant of the Creevna ash and it is said that parts of this tree were taken to America by emigrating Irish.

The ash tree is also sacred in the Norse and Germanic traditions, with many believing the world tree Yggdrasil to be an ash. Arising from a golden seed, Yggdrasil's three roots reach into three wells that feed all life in the nine worlds. A dragon named Nidhog nibbles at one of the roots while an eagle sits in the boughs with a hawk called Veðrfölnir between its eyes. Between the dragon and the eagle runs a squirrel named Ratatoskr, which gossips and causes trouble between the two. There are also four sacred deer, Dáinn, Dvalinn,

## WATER CORRESPONDENCE
Wells · Life · Protection

Duneyrr, and Duraþrór, which eat the fresh leaves as they grow.

Later in the Norse creation story, Odin the All Father and his brothers, Vili and Ve, create Ask, the first man, from one of the ash tree's branches. The first woman, Embla, comes from the elm. Mirroring this, ash also appears in the creation story of the Abenaki people, in New Hampshire. After failing to create a suitable man from stone, the creator makes man from an ash branch. In another version of the Abenaki story, a mythic character called Gluskabe shoots arrows into ash trees and people emerge from the trees.

Many centuries earlier, the ancient Greeks believed that nature deities—nymphs known as Meliae, rather than humans—came from ash trees. This is reminiscent of an English folk tale collected by Ruth Tongue in the 1970s, which she calls *The Green Ladies of One Tree Hill*. In this story, paying homage to the spirits that live in three ash trees on a hill on the outskirts of a farm is essential to ensure they will continue to protect the farm. In parts of Scandinavia—Sweden in particular—these deities take the form of an *Askafroa* (Ash Wife) but are more malevolent. In fact, it was considered bad luck to cut down a tree in which an Ash Wife lived. To ensure the Ash Wife did not harm the community, a ritual was carried out each year to appease her.

*In the Norse creation story, Odin the All Father and his brothers, Vili and Ve, create Ask, the first man, from one of the ash tree's branches.*

In the UK, from the Iron Age to the end of the Anglo-Saxon Period (*ca.* 800 BCE–1066 CE), ash was used to make spears and shields, while milk pails and churns fashioned from ash were thought to protect milk from witches and fairies who might try to curdle it. Ash was also used to make everyday items and in folk medicine. For example, to this day, mulled cider in a cup made of ash, known as the wassailing cup, is passed around the community before the remainder is poured on the apple tree's roots to bless the tree for the coming year.

Ash was also thought to cure many ills, from warts to congenital conditions, perhaps another nod to the source of life with which the tree is frequently associated. A common ritual involved passing a wounded child through a cleft in the trunk of an ash tree. The cleft would then be bound and sealed, and as the ash healed, so did the child. To cure cattle, a live shrew would be left in the cleft and sealed in instead.

Ash seeds were considered portentous, and in Yorkshire, England, carters would hang ash keys from their horse's bridle to ward off flies and protect them on their journey. They were also thought to divine good or bad years for English royalty: If the ash tree failed to produce seeds one year, this foretold a royal death within the year. This is said to have happened in 1648—one year later, in 1649, Charles I was executed for high treason and the monarchy was briefly abolished in England.

Another divination practice using ash calls for young women to take the leaves from an ash twig with an even number of leaves—known as an "even ash"— and place them in their gloves. Then whoever they meet first on their walk that day will be their true love.

> Look to the ash for its healing powers.
>
> ———
> Affirmation

# GOLDEN WATTLE
*Acacia pycnantha*

## *A flexible tree of cultural and spiritual importance*

The golden wattle belongs to the *Acacia* genus of trees that includes over a thousand different species. These are native to Africa, South America, and Australasia, and there are both naturally occurring species and cultivated varieties in the genus.

A member of the pea family, Fabaceae, the golden wattle is a small evergreen tree that is more often referred to as a shrub, but some species, such as the black wattle (*Acacia mearnsii*), can grow up to 33 feet (10 m) tall. The golden wattle has leaves that hang down and are known as phyllodes, a type of stem that is wide and flat like a leaf. Among the phyllodes, the flowers range from the palest yellow to the deepest gold and form small clusters of pom-poms along the branches.

In Australia, acacias are known as wattles. The golden wattle is a deeply spiritual and sacred tree for First Nations peoples, with links to their ancestors and stories of the Everywhen or Dreamtime. But acacias did not become known as wattle trees until 1810, with the name thought to come from the Old English *watul*, meaning "to weave." This word referred to any tree flexible enough to use as a building material and therefore woven into walls and fences. Both the Indigenous peoples and settlers in Australia used wattles for this purpose. In the case of buildings, it is thought that the black wattle is most likely to have been used.

The golden wattle has been the national flower of Australia since 1988 and can be found across the southeastern Australian territories. It flowers from August to September and is considered to be a sign of spring. Symbolizing remembrance, the wattle flower appears on stamps and currency in Australia, as well as on some medals awarded for honors. National Wattle Day has been held on September 1 since

## WATER CORRESPONDENCE
Flexibility • Memory • Transport

1992, and on this day wattles are planted and communities come together to learn about the history of the wattle tree.

Although the acacia has strong links with Australia, it is thought that the trees originated in Egypt and that the genus name comes from the Greek word *akakis*, meaning "point," in reference to the spikes from which the leaves grow. In ancient Egypt, ships were of great importance for transport and trading, but also for ceremonial burials. The Greek historian and geographer Herodotus, writing around 500 BCE, notes in his *Histories II* that Egyptian boats were built with short planks of acacia in staggered rows like bricks, with dowels to hold them together and a caulking of papyrus. Small boats were frequently made in this way since it was easier than sourcing the more durable cedar of Lebanon (*Cedrus libani*).

The acacia also features in the Egyptian myth of Isis and Osiris. The children of Geb (the Earth god) and Nut (the sky goddess) were Isis, Osiris, Set, and Nephthys, with Isis and Osiris considered the first royal couple of Egypt, inheriting the throne from the sun god Ra. Osiris's rule was prosperous and successful, and his brother Set became jealous and contrived to rid himself of Osiris. He made a casket that would only fit Osiris and created a game in which he asked everyone to see if they could fit inside. Osiris was, of course, the only one to fit in the casket, and Set sealed him inside and threw him in the Nile. Osiris suffocated and floated downriver. In some versions of the myth, Osiris's body is retrieved and he is buried beneath an acacia tree.

*Golden wattle is a deeply spiritual and sacred tree for First Nations peoples, with links to their ancestors and stories of the Everywhen and Dreamtime.*

The wattle is important as a food source for several insect and animal species, but has also been a good source of protein for humans. Although part of the Indigenous Australian diet for many centuries, it has more recently become a favorite of the modern Australian food industry, known as the bushfood industry, which emerged in the 1970s. This industry encourages and sells native Australian species as food, and promotes ground wattle seeds for flavoring ice cream and for use in wattle damper bread, a traditional bread cooked on hot coals. In North America, the people of the Cahuilla and Pima tribes also use acacia in cakes or simply eat the seeds raw. Not all acacia species are edible, though, so don't eat any acacia plant unless you know for certain that it is one of those that you can safely eat.

Acacia bark is highly valued for its tannins, which means it can be used as a natural tanning agent in lotions. The tannins have also been found to protect the skin and increase the length of time the tanning agent works. This has resulted in 5 million acres (2 million hectares) of commercial plantations across the world. Acacias have many other applications, however, and for thousands of years were used to make tools, boats, clubs, spears, boomerangs, shields, and, more recently, furniture.

## Look to the golden wattle for versatility.

Affirmation

# CEIBA
*Ceiba pentandra*

## *A spiritual tree believed to underpin all life*

The most well-known species in this genus is *Ceiba pentandra*, known as the silk-cotton tree or kapok in English, *kankantrie* in Afro-Surinamese, and *fromager* in French. Native to Mexico, South and Central America, the Caribbean, and West Africa, it reaches a height of almost 262 feet (80 m) with a trunk up to 10 feet (3 m) in diameter.

The buttress roots anchor the tree and begin around a quarter of the way up the trunk, reminiscent of a tent's guy ropes. Below ground, the roots extend almost as far as the canopy, which can be over 200 feet (60 m) wide. Large thorns grow on the trunk and branches, although there are also smaller, smooth-barked species in the genus.

*Ceiba pentandra* has palmate leaves with up to nine leaflets fanning out from each stem. Once the leaves drop, clusters of small, yellow flowers appear, followed by hundreds of large seedpods, all containing a fluffy, cotton-like fiber.

Another striking kapok species, *Bombax ceiba*, native to Asia and northern Australia, has large, crimson flowers.

The fibrous seeds have huge commercial value and have been used for centuries. The Indigenous Amazonians use the cotton fibers to wrap the ends of blow darts for hunting food. They have also been used to stuff toys, furniture, mattresses, upholstery, and car seats. However, *Ceiba pentandra* is highly flammable and so has fallen out of favor for these purposes. It is very buoyant, though, and was used to fill life jackets until the mid-1900s.

The ceiba supports a variety of wildlife, including birds, mammals, bees, and bats. The greater short-nosed fruit bat (*Cynopterus sphinx*) and Indian flying fox (*Pteropus giganteus*) are the tree's main pollinators. Vines and bromeliads grow in the branches, and tree frogs raise tadpoles within the pools of water that collect in the bromeliads.

## WATER CORRESPONDENCE
Frogs • Buoyancy • Rivers

The ancient Maya knew *Ceiba pentandra* as the *Yax Che*, meaning "first tree," and like other trees in world mythology, it is considered the tree that connects and supports all life. Four ceiba trees support the corners of the universe and facilitate communication between three worlds: the Underworld in the roots, the human world of the trunk, and the upperworld of the branches, which holds the thirteen levels of heaven. It is believed that the tree would carry souls to heaven. Today, the Indigenous Tikuna people of Colombia's Amazon rainforest believe that when the first tree fell, it became the Amazon River, and from it sprang new life.

*Ceiba pentandra* has a dark side, however. In Cuban folklore it is associated with the Güijes, river-dwelling, goblin-like creatures that guard rivers and trees. Offerings can be made to the Güijes and they can be summoned by circling the ceiba tree twelve times, but care must be taken since these beings are known to cause mischief and are feared by lone travelers.

The genus name *Ceiba* means "boat" in the language of the Taíno people of the Caribbean, who carved canoes from the trunks. In St. Lucia, rituals are carried out for new fishing boats to keep the owner safe. In some cases, a ceiba thorn is hidden behind the tiller near the rudder to act as the boat's guardian. The thorn should never be placed in the bow and no one must know it's there. If you build a boat from an odd number of ceiba pieces, it will be the fastest vessel. There is a trade-off, though, as these boats capsize easily and it is thought that using ceiba in this way means you've made a pact with the Devil. In the past, making a boat from the ceiba tree would lead to ostracization by the community and, at some point, the Devil would call in his dues.

*The Indigenous Tikuna people of Colombia's Amazon rainforest believe that when the first ceiba tree fell, it became the Amazon River.*

In Trinidad and Tobago, the tree is said to be the castle of Bazil, a demonic being of death who was once tricked by a carpenter called Papa Le Bois so the demon could not collect his soul at death. To achieve this, Papa Le Bois carved seven rooms in the ceiba tree, one on top of the other, and when Bazil came to claim his soul, Papa le Bois told him that he needed to see his life's work first. Bazil agreed and Papa Le Bois showed him through the rooms, unlocking each door as they went until they reached the last room. Here, Papa Le Bois said that only he was allowed to see the wonder of this room. Naturally, Bazil demanded to see the room, and Papa Le Bois made a show of reluctantly opening the door. Bazil rushed in and Papa Le Bois quickly locked him in. But with death a prisoner, the island became overpopulated and, after seven long years, Papa Le Bois was forced by the community to open the door and meet his fate.

The soft, light wood of *Ceiba pentandra* makes it unsuitable for building structures or making tools and furniture. It is this, along with the lore of the devil's castle, that has kept it reasonably well protected. Now, however, the wood is being used to make pallets faster than it can regenerate. Let us hope that Bazil can help the ceiba.

> Look to the ceiba tree to remind you of the trade-off in all transactions.
>
> Affirmation

# COCO DE MER

*Lodoicea maldivica*

## *A tree of wonder that is steeped in mystery*

The coco de mer, which translates roughly as "sea coconut," is a tree full of passion and intrigue. A member of the palm family Arecaceae, this fascinating tree only grows on the islands of Praslin and Curieuse in the Seychelles. Until around three hundred years ago, the coco de mer's home was not well known across the world because unless you lived where the tree grew, you would only ever see the nut washed up on a shore far away from its original location.

The coco de mer's nut is famous for being the shape and size of a woman's buttocks, which prompted the Greeks to name the tree *Lodoicea callipyge*, the latter word meaning "beautiful rump." Furthermore, the other side of the nut resembles a rounded pregnant belly. The nut is the largest seed of any plant and can weigh around 90 pounds (41 kg). The only way the tree can reproduce is if the nut remains where it falls, allowing it to germinate and take root. Some of the fallen nuts are inevitably washed into the sea, where they sink under their own weight. The tough husk biodegrades underwater and the inside of the nut starts to ferment, releasing gases. The nut then rises to the surface and eventually washes up on various shores.

The tree itself can grow to a height of about 100 feet (30 m). A dense canopy of palmate foliage hides the fruit as it grows and ripens, changing from green to dark brown. The female trees produce the fruit, and the male trees bear large catkins that are unmistakably phallic. We are still not completely sure how the coco de mer reproduces. In some stories, the trees are said to walk across the forest floor to find each other, while other tales say that on stormy nights the trees bend together and mate. But lore tells us that you must never see them do this, for the sight will strike you blind.

Praslin, the second-largest island in the Seychelles archipelago, remained

## WATER CORRESPONDENCE
Journeys • Fertility • The Sea

undiscovered until 1768, when French explorers finally found the home of the mysterious nut. Before this, the unknown location of the trees led to many tales, one of which was that they grew on the ocean floor, since sailors would see the nuts rising to the surface of the ocean and assume there to be a forest of coco de mer trees beneath the waves.

The lore then evolved to encompass a monstrous underwater bird named the Garuda, which was said to live underwater in the tree. It was claimed that the bird would emerge from the water to hunt elephants and tigers. Any ships caught in the backwash of this rising bird were doomed, and the sailors would also fall prey to the hungry beast.

The coco de mer also appears in the creation stories of Praslin. It is said that the creator god sealed the song of creation inside a huge shell and then hid it at the bottom of the ocean. The song drifted through the ocean and reached the ears of a water goddess who followed the sound and found the nut. She pried the nut open and shared its secrets with her lover, the Earth god. The creator vowed to strike them down and, terrified, they hid in the dense forests of the world.

When the creator found them and saw their fierce love, he took pity on them, turning them into two separate trees, one male and one female. These trees are now known as coco de mer. The creator then took the trees as well as the mountain on which they stood and placed them in the ocean, where they became the island of Praslin. As a result, it's said that the scent of coco de mer flowers holds the secret of love.

The rarity and unknown location of the tree meant that the nut was, and still is, highly prized. The story goes that in 1602, after the Dutch admiral

> *We are still not completely sure how the coco de mer reproduces. . . . Some tales say that on stormy nights the trees bend together and mate.*

Wolfert Hermansson helped the Sultan of Banten defend the port on Java, in Indonesia, against Portuguese attack, the Sultan gave him the coco de mer nut by way of thanks. This nut was apparently later sold to Rudolf II, the Holy Roman Emperor, for four thousand gold florins—about US $750,000 in today's money.

Around the same time, if the nuts washed up on the shores of the Maldives, they were said to belong to the king. If you sold or were found in possession of one, you could be put to death. The nut became popular in royal households across the world and was often carved and lined with gold and silver gilding. The nut is still very popular with royalty to this day. Indeed, in 2011, Prince William and Princess Catherine of the British royal family were presented with a coco de mer fruit at the end of their ten-day honeymoon in the Seychelles.

Today the coco de mer is home to the rare Seychelles black parrot (*Coracopsis barklyi*), and the tree and its nuts are protected by strict export regulations. The Vallée de Mai on Praslin, where it grows, is a UNESCO World Heritage Site, the smallest in the world.

# Look to the coco de mer to embrace the mysteries in life.

Affirmation

# MAGIC GUARRI
*Euclea divinorum*

## *A tenacious and sacred tree offering healing and protection*

The magic guarri, sometimes referred to as the diamond-leaved euclea, is native to eastern and southern Africa. It thrives in the Lowveld, a subtropical woodland found in the south of the continent. It seeks out waterlogged sites, floodplains, and even termite mounds, and it also grows close to rivers and streams.

The young trees have smooth, gray bark that cracks as they reach maturity. Multiple stems rise from one root base, and the round evergreen crown of the tree carries slim, leathery leaves with crinkled edges. The magic guarri rarely reaches more than 26 feet (8 m) in height, and its sweet-scented, bell-like, yellow flowers bloom in clusters from late summer to early winter. The fruit is a small, round berry that holds a single seed and changes from green to a deep, almost black-purple as it ripens.

Magic guarri is used in many ways, including for tools, as food, and to promote good health. But be careful: Magic guarri berries resemble the berries of certain toxic plants. Don't proceed if there is any doubt that the berries you want to use are in fact magic guarri. If you take a small twig from the tree and peel off the bark at one end, the flesh inside will fray, producing an effective toothbrush—unsurprisingly, it is sometimes known as the toothbrush tree. The bark and roots can be used to make a red/brown dye for clothing or tanning leather, while the berries can produce a pink or brown ink. The wood is also used for making tool handles and building materials; however, it is never used as a fuel, since this is considered to be very bad luck and disrespectful to what is a magical tree for many.

The berries are a favorite of the silvery-cheeked hornbill (*Bycanistes brevis*), but as a food source for humans, the berries are not that appetizing. However, they can be made into a juice,

## WATER CORRESPONDENCE

Divination • Adaptability • Floodplains

jelly, and vinegar. The roots are also occasionally used in the fermentation process when brewing beer. Branches of the tree can be placed over meat or pails of milk to preserve them, since the scent of the leaves deters flies.

The Latin name for the tree, *Euclea divinorum*, comes from the name of the Greek goddess Eukleaia (or Eucleia), a goddess of honor and glory. She is a chaste goddess and one of the attendants of Aphrodite. Along with *divinorum*, *Euclea* implies that the magic guarri is an honored and renowned tree. This is confirmed by the beliefs of the Indigenous Zulu tribes, who honor the magic guarri for its healing properties. The tree is used by the sangomas, the revered healers of the Zulu tribes, to help them connect with the spiritual realm during healing rituals.

The tree's traditional medicinal uses are many and varied. The dried root can be made into a paste to be used on external wounds, dermatitis, and a variety of skin disorders, from scabies to leprosy. It can also be used to treat snakebites and headaches, abdominal pain, toothache, and earache. This is likely due to phytochemicals within the root, which have been found to have antinociceptive properties, meaning they can block the perception of pain through the sensory neurons. The root can also be used as a purgative or laxative and is known to be particularly effective at ridding the gut of parasites.

Perhaps because of its many healing properties, the magic guarri is also regarded as a tool of protection and apotropaic magic (magic that averts bad luck or evil influences). Much like Europe's hawthorn and birch, a magic guarri branch can be hung above or by the door of a home to keep away witches and malevolent forces. Similarly, carrying a sprig of the tree is said to bring you good luck.

*The tree is used by the sangomas, the revered healers of the Zulu tribes, to help them connect with the spiritual realm during healing rituals.*

The waxy coating of the magic guarri's leaves means the tree retains water well and does not dry out. As a result, it can be used to track animals. Trackers note that if the dew on the tree's branches has been disturbed, then an animal has potentially passed by, brushing against it and dispersing the water that collected there. These properties also make the branches of the tree excellent for putting out fires.

A Y-shaped stick of magic guarri can be used for dowsing. By holding the two ends of the Y, one in each hand, the dowser walks across the land where they are looking for water. If the end of the stick dips downward, this indicates there is a water source below ground.

The tree can also predict drought and will warn other trees of this. If the tree is starved of water, it will release a pheromone that lets other trees know they must conserve this precious resource. The tree also pushes tannins into its leaves, making them extremely bitter, to deter animals from eating them. In this way, even during a drought, the magic guarri can send up new shoots from the base that will not be eaten by passing wildlife.

> Look to the magic guarri for the gift of prophecy.
>
> ———
>
> Affirmation

Chapter 3

# AIR: TREES OF RESILIENCE

The Air element represents intellect, creativity, freedom, life force, and spiritual energy passing around us or through us. It is an ethereal element that we can't see but need every day. The very essence of trees is passed to us through the air when they convert the sun's energy into vital oxygen, while the phytoncides they emit help regulate our hormones, build strong immune systems, support our circulatory and nervous systems, and in turn alleviate symptoms of anxiety. The trees in this chapter offer stories of poets and muses, aromas that induce prophetic dreams, cures for respiratory conditions, and those that have withstood extinction events.

# WILLOW
*Salix*

## *Pliable and with healing powers, the willow inspires creativity*

The goat willow (*Salix caprea*) is a common species of willow found in Europe and West and Central Asia. It rarely grows taller than 30 feet (10 m), and the fluffy catkins that bloom in early spring have earned it the nickname pussy willow, since they are said to look like tiny cat's paws. The male catkins are silky soft, gray, and rounded until they turn yellow with pollen, and provide much-needed early nectar for insects. The female catkins are green and thinner than their male counterparts. When the female catkins are pollinated, they produce downy seeds.

The name *willow* comes from the Old English for "pliable" or "willing," *wiðig* (pronounced "withy"), a nod to its use in woven fences and basket making. It is thought that "goat willow" comes from the first known illustration of the tree, which appears in a sixteenth-century herbal called the *Kreuter Buch* (Book of herbs) by German botanist Hieronymus Bock. In this illustration, there are goats grazing on the tree, and it is noted that the goat willow was often used by goat herders to graze their flocks.

In America, the *Salix discolor* species is also known as pussy willow. Internationally renowned storyteller Tchin, who has Indigenous Siksika and Narragansett heritage, tells the tale of how the rabbit, who once had long legs, a long tail, and very short ears, came to look the way he does. One spring, Rabbit saw the willow buds and wanted to eat them, but they were too high up on the tree. Instead, Rabbit ate some grass and began to think of how lovely it would be if it snowed, so he danced and wished for snow, and it started falling.

Soon the snow was so deep he was level with the willow buds. He ate his fill and fell asleep in the branches of the tree. When he woke, the sun was high and had melted all the snow, leaving

## AIR CORRESPONDENCE
### Music · Poetry · Spirits

Rabbit stuck in the tree. As he tried to climb down, he hung on to a branch with his tail, but it broke and he fell to the ground. Rabbit's ears stretched as they caught on every branch, and his legs bent and shortened when he landed. This is why Rabbit now looks the way he does and why the remnants of his tail still hang from the willow tree.

The Doctrine of Signatures—the concept that a plant will cure the illness that corresponds with what it looks like or where it grows—suggests that because the willow loves damp environments, it will cure any illness made worse by the damp, such as rheumatism. On this occasion, the theory is correct, as we now know that willow bark contains salicylic acid, a constituent of aspirin, and so has pain-relieving and anti-inflammatory properties that would alleviate rheumatic pain.

Chewing willow twigs also offers relief from headaches. Two tenth-century healing texts suggest ways to relieve pain with willow bark. The Anglo-Saxon book *Lacnunga* (Remedies) prescribes using willow bark as part of a salve for a headache, while *Bald's Leechbook* suggests green willow bark boiled with honey to alleviate spleen pain. Be very careful if you use willow bark as a painkiller, though, because it can have painful side effects, and do not use willow bark at all if you are pregnant or have kidney disease.

Willow is closely associated with protection, and in Christianity, goat willow is often worn as a cross on Palm Sunday. Sometimes these crosses are placed in houses and kept until the following year. They are said to protect against disease, storms, and bad luck. This has given rise to the name palm willow. Willow was also placed among garden crops for a good harvest, hung over doorways to repel witches, and used by miners as amulets to guard against accidents belowground.

The willow is also a tree of grief in many places. In China, during the Qingming Festival, which welcomes in the spring and honors the ancestors—by clearing their graves and tombs, for example—willow is hung above doorways to ensure the souls of the dead do not wander into homes. In Louisiana, if a willow tree, probably the black willow (*Salix nigra*), grew large enough to cast a shadow the size of a

> *In Slavic lore the willow is associated with a devil-like character named Rokita who lives in the tree and is said to be connected with the Underworld.*

grave, there was likely to be a death in the family, while in the Celtic tradition, white willows (*Salix alba*) are seen as grieving trees. Willows were planted at Celtic burial sites so the spirit of the deceased could rise into the sapling, acting as a psychopomp (a conductor of souls to the afterlife) and confirming its association with the Underworld.

The white willow is important to the bards in the Celtic tradition and is considered to be the tree of femininity and the moon. For the Druids, the willow tree is the source of poetry and music. A harp made of willow, known as Brian Boru's harp, is held by Trinity College Dublin and is believed to date from the fourteenth or fifteenth century. This harp appears on the Irish coat of arms. Indeed, willow is said to have the ability to inspire poets, musicians, and bards alike. It is believed the soul of the willow in the harp speaks through the music, and in this way the willow takes the form of words that dance in the air.

The willow is certainly a complex tree, sometimes inspirational and sometimes holding dark folkloric beings. In Slavic lore, the willow is associated with a devil-like character named Rokita who lives in the tree and is said to be connected with the Underworld. One old saying states: "Ellum [elm] do grieve, oak he do hate, willow do walk if you travel late," while on Exmoor in southwestern England, there are reports of walkers being followed by willow trees.

## Look to the willow to bring creativity into your life.

Affirmation

# BAY LAUREL
*Laurus nobilis*

## *A noble tree signifying honor and success*

Most commonly referred to as the bay laurel or bay tree, *Laurus nobilis* is a popular culinary herb, prized for its scent and healing properties. Also known as royal or sweet bay, this tree has been an important part of European ritual and ceremony since the eighth century BCE. With glossy, dark green to black oval leaves, it forms clusters of small, pale green-yellow flowers, which turn to black fruit known as bayberries in the fall.

Bay laurel is associated with the Greek myth of Apollo and Daphne. Daphne was a river nymph on whom the sun god Apollo had set his sights. She pleaded with her father, the river god Peneus, to hide her from her pursuer. In some versions of the myth, Peneus grants the request and in others he turns away, ignoring the situation and leaving the Earth goddess Gaia to intervene. In either case, Daphne is transformed into a bay tree. Still intent on possessing the nymph, Apollo takes sprigs from Daphne's branches and wears them as a wreath. From this point on, the laurel wreath came to represent Apollo.

The laurel finds itself once more in the presence of the gods in the ancient Greek city of Delphi, now a UNESCO World Heritage Site. Here, a temple once stood on Mount Parnassus, a limestone spur at the end of the Pindus Mountains in central Greece. It is said that Zeus sent two eagles to find the center of the Earth and they alighted at Delphi.

The oracle and priestess Pythia, who resided there between the eighth and fourth centuries BCE, was said to speak the words of Apollo and was consulted in matters of law, war, politics, and farming. A laurel grove surrounded the temple at Delphi and within it was the spirit of Apollo. In order to induce prophetic dreams, it is recorded that Pythia chewed the leaves and inhaled the scent of the laurel tree.

## AIR CORRESPONDENCE
Prophecy • Nymphs • Redolence

While laurel lacks the chemicals to induce hallucinations, Giulia Frigerio, in a paper from 2023 titled "Apolline Divination," argues that this represents a deeper human connection with the tree, embodied by a neural response to the smell of its leaves.

> *The ancient Greeks used the laurel wreath to crown Olympic champions and master poets, a tradition that the Romans continued.*

The ancient Greeks used the laurel wreath to crown Olympic champions and master poets, a tradition that the Romans continued, since they saw the bay laurel as representative of honor, fame, and success. The Romans awarded laurel wreath crowns to warriors, doctors, and, famously, emperors. The laurel wreath as a representation of victory was used in 1815, when Napoleon was defeated at the Battle of Waterloo. The mail coaches that thundered through Britain, carrying news of victory, were decorated with laurel. Still to this day, the laurel is used as an award for outstanding achievement, with the Olympic laurel being introduced in 2016 by the International Olympic Committee as an award for those who have "made significant achievements in education, culture, development, and peace through sport."

Bay is also considered to be a tree of protection. A bay tree planted by the door would keep away the plague, a belief that can be traced back to the ancient Greeks, who would hang a sprig above the door of someone who was ill. A laurel leaf held in the mouth was said to provide protection against maleficent forces and, in some areas of England, shepherds would place bay wreaths under their caps in a storm to protect them from lightning.

Throughout history, bay has been used for a variety of medicinal and practical purposes. During the medieval period in England, it was used in various salves for eye complaints such as styes, while modern folk uses include making a tea with the leaves, which have antispasmodic properties and can be an aid in digestion. The leaves have been shown to possess antiseptic qualities and, if chewed in small quantities, can not only clean the teeth and gums but can then be placed on bites and stings to alleviate inflammation. The essential oil can be used as a muscle and joint rub.

A practical rather than medicinal application during the seventeenth century involved boiling bayberries in water for several hours to produce a wax, which gathered on the surface of the water and could be filtered off to use as tapers. When lit, the tapers gave off a fragrant smell that was the direct opposite of the more easily available tallow (animal fat). It was a labor-intensive process, though, with 15 pounds (7 kg) of bayberries providing just 1 pound (450 g) of wax, and so these tapers were saved for special occasions.

Cousin to the bay laurel is the cherry laurel (*Prunus laurocerasus*), known in the United States as English laurel. Used as a fast-growing hedging plant, this laurel also has leaves similar to the bay laurel, but its flowers cluster on stems that grow vertically, and the leaves and fruit pips contain small amounts of cyanide. While there are no reported deaths due to cherry laurel, it is not advised to consume any part of this plant. It has, however, had its place in culinary history and was once used in the seventeenth century in custards and puddings, as the leaves gave desserts an almond flavor.

> **Look to the laurel as a witness to your achievements.**
>
> Affirmation

# GINKGO
*Ginkgo biloba*

## *An ancient tree capable of withstanding disaster*

The ginkgo tree is a unique species dating back 120 million years. It is the one remaining species in its order, Ginkgoales, and for a long time it was only found in the Chinese provinces of Zhejiang and Guizhou.

The tree is deciduous, with bright green, fan-shaped leaves in summer that turn deep gold in the fall. Male trees produce flowers, and the females bear round, yellow, fruit-like structures that contain a large seed. Vertical spikes of small, green flowers produce pollen in spring, and in the fall, the "fruits" have the appearance of a soft, yellow-green golf ball. The unpleasant smell of the "fruits" is not as inviting as this tree's aesthetics. Ginkgo trees are resilient to air pollution in cities and become dormant in low light. The tree grows best in warmer climates, where it can reach a height of around 82 feet (25 m).

The ginkgo is a tree of many names. In China the ginkgo tree is known as Yā jiǎo shù (duck foot tree), due to the shape of its leaves, and Yín xìng (silver apricot) because of its "fruits." Its longevity and the fact that it takes around thirty-five years to reach maturity has also given it the name Yéye sūnzǐ shù (grandfather-grandson tree).

In Japan many existing specimens are over a thousand years old, with the oldest being 3,500 years old. No wonder there is speculation that such an ancient tree may be the missing link between conifers and ferns. Indeed, the ginkgo is sometimes called the maidenhair tree due to its similarities with the maidenhair fern (*Adiantum* species). It was Buddhist monks who brought the tree to Japan and Korea in the twelfth century, where the ginkgo became a sacred tree planted outside Taoist and Buddhist temples. Today, it is often found at Shinto shrines and is regarded as *shinboku*, a tree that holds local nature spirits and ancient wisdom.

## AIR CORRESPONDENCE

Ancient Wisdom • Respiratory Health • Resilience

Engelbert Kaempfer, a seventeenth-century German botanist, encountered the tree in Nagasaki while working for

> *The ginkgo is often found at Shinto shrines and is regarded as shinboku, a tree that holds local nature spirits.*

the Dutch East India Company, and brought the seeds from Japan to Europe. Cor Kwant, writing for *The Ginkgo Pages* blog, theorizes that the modern name for the tree evolved from a mistake made by Engelbert Kaempfer in his notes. The tree was known as ginkyo in Japan (*gin*, meaning "silver," and *kyō*, meaning "apricot"). When Kaempfer wrote this down, the *y* looked like a *g*, and the typesetter for his subsequent book recorded the tree as the ginkgo.

The ginkgo nut, the seed found inside the fruit structure, was once a rare delicacy and has been a food source since the second century BCE. Due to its rarity, for many centuries the nut was given as a gift to royalty. There are records from the fifteenth century of ginkgo nuts being used in Sadō (also spelled Chadō, meaning "the way of tea"). Known in the West as the Japanese tea ceremony, it is an art form dedicated to presenting matcha tea for drinking.

During the eighteenth century, the nuts were consumed as an appetizer or digestif, usually accompanied by sake (rice wine). Today, they are often eaten roasted at Chinese festivals in the fall. Ginkgo nuts should be consumed with caution, however, as they are considered poisonous: eating even roasted seeds may cause seizures and eating fresh seeds may cause death. Even gingko leaf extract, taken in typical quantities, may cause side effects. The oil from the nuts is also known to cause skin irritation.

In medicine, ginkgo nuts and leaves have been used for hundreds of years. The *Běn Cáo Gāng Mù*, a sixteenth-century encyclopedia written by Li Shizhen, is considered to be one of the most comprehensive compilations of natural medicine of its time and still forms the basis for Chinese medicine today. It suggests the nuts can be used for respiratory conditions and bladder complaints. More popular uses include using it as a stimulant to increase circulation and concentration. These properties have led to a sharp increase in consumption of the nuts in the West, and in one plantation in South Carolina, ten million trees are harvested by machine each year. The trees are then cut down to their roots every five years and regenerate again. This specially adapted tree survives this treatment by storing energy in a part of the roots called a lignotuber, allowing them to regrow and produce crops.

Fossils of ginkgo seeds have been found that date back to before several mass extinction events. The most recent evidence that the ginkgo tree is a survivor comes from August 6, 1945, the date of the atomic bombing of Hiroshima. While all around them the buildings and flora and fauna were razed to the ground, six ginkgo trees survived. These trees are known as Hibakujumoku (survivor trees). Trees at the temples of Hosen-ji, Josei-ji, Myojo-in, and Anraku-ji, as well as Shukkeien Garden and the site of the former Senda Elementary School, all stand within 1.5 miles (2 km) of the epicenter of the blast, and each tree bears a plaque stating: A-BOMBED TREE. Some still have scorch marks on their trunks.

The communities rebuilt the buildings and temples around these trees, and each fall, Mayors for Peace, an international network dedicated to peace, collects the seeds from the trees that survived the Hiroshima bombing and distributes them around the world. As a result, the ginkgo tree is considered the "bearer of hope" in Japan.

# Look to the ginkgo for the transitory nature of life.

Affirmation

# SUGAR MAPLE
*Acer saccharum*

## *A beautiful tree of plenty and sustenance*

The iconic sugar maple can be found in the hardwood forests of eastern Canada and the United States. Intrinsically linked to Canadian culture through its appearance on the flag of Canada, the sugar maple is known throughout the world for the sweet syrup that is derived from its sap. The maple leaf was first used as an emblem of Canada in 1868 on the coat of arms for the provinces of Ontario and Quebec. The project to find a national flag was prompted by the country's prime minister, Lester B. Pearson, in 1960, and the winning design, by George Stanley, has been used as Canada's flag since 1965.

Without its leaves, the sugar maple is identifiable by its pointed, brown leaf buds, found in threes at the end of each twig. The yellow flowers grow in clusters, which turn into pairs of samaras (winged seeds) that hang from the branches. The leaves of the maple have a distinctive, palmate shape and are around 8 in (20 cm) wide. The sugar maple is deciduous, and the fall foliage turns a variety of colors, from deep yellow through orange to bright red.

Maple syrup has formed an important part of the diet and traditions of First Nations peoples. For thousands of years, in late winter, the tribes in the area collected the sap by making gashes in the trees and boiling it down to create a syrup. A small pail made from birch wood, called a mokuk, was once used to collect the sap. Metal pails and drilled holes in the trees have since replaced the traditional method; however, the importance of this harvest has remained.

Sugaring, or sugaring off, lasting around six weeks between late winter and mid-spring, is the name given to the season in which the maple sap can be collected. Freezing temperatures at night and thawing temperatures in the day are the conditions essential for collecting the sap. When the pools of

## AIR CORRESPONDENCE

Balance • Communication • Ancestral Knowledge

snowmelt begin to fill with frogs and frog spawn, it is time to collect the last of the sap in what the Indigenous peoples of the area call the frog run. At the end of the season, a boiled and reduced syrup is offered to the Great Spirit by way of honoring them and giving thanks. The whole process is a community activity.

> *The tradition of sugaring off parties was quickly adopted by settlers, and today they herald the spring.*

When settlers arrived in Canada, the Algonquians taught them how to tap the trees, and from there the maple syrup industry grew. Quebec is considered to be the maple syrup region of the country, producing 90 percent of Canada's domestic supply and 74 percent of the international supply. It takes around 40 gallons (150 L) of sap to make 1 gallon (4 L) of maple syrup,

and over 17 million gallons (64 million L) of syrup are produced each year.

The tradition of sugaring off parties was quickly adopted by settlers, and today they herald the spring. These celebrations have taken on a festival feel, with maple syrup being made into "sugar on snow," or maple taffy, in a process that involves pouring boiled maple syrup onto fresh snow, allowing it to cool, and then eating it. People can visit *cabanes à sucre* (sugar shacks) to eat sugar on snow, which it is often served with donuts to dip in the syrup, with pickles and black coffee to cut through the sweetness of the taffy.

Many stories surround maple trees and the spirits that are associated with them. One such story comes from the Anishinaabe peoples, an Indigenous group living around the Great Lakes in Canada and the United States, and which includes the Ojibwe, Algonquin, and Potawatomi peoples. Contemporary storyteller Zhaawnong Webb, an Anishinaabe-nini (man), tells the story of Nanabozho, the great creator god and trickster from the Anishinaabe tradition. The story tells of how one winter, the people of the area were starving and the maple tree saw this and took pity on them. It promised them that, no matter what time of year, if they were in need, they could break a branch off the tree, and a thick, sweet, sustaining syrup would run from it. From that point on, the Anishinaabe people could drink the sap of the maple whenever they wanted.

One day, Nanabozho decided to visit the Anishinaabe, but he could find no one when he arrived. They were not at their usual tasks, nor in their homes. He went into the woods to find them, and what he saw shocked him. There in the forest, all the Anishinaabe people were lying on their backs with the thick, brown sap of the maple pouring into their mouths. Nanabozho admonished the Anishinaabe, telling them they would become lazy and fat if they continued in this way and that they showed the trees disrespect with their overconsumption. He took water from the river and poured it into the maple trees, so that now the Anishinaabe would have to boil down the sap to have the sweet syrup. As a result, they would have to work for the maple tree's gifts, learning to value and respect the tree and work together as a community.

## Look to the maple for the sweetness in life.

Affirmation

# WOLLEMI PINE
*Wollemia nobilis*

*An ancient tree that has stood the test of time*

The Wollemi pine is considered a living fossil and was thought to be extinct until a chance discovery in the early 1990s. Part of the Araucariaceae family, the tree is native to the sandstone slot canyons of the Blue Mountains in New South Wales, Australia. It is related to conifers, and its closest living relative is the monkey puzzle tree *(Araucaria araucana)*. Both are now sought after as ornamental specimens in arboreta and gardens across the world.

The story of the Wollemi pine is millions of years old. It is thought to date from the late Neoproterozoic Era, around 550 million years ago, when Australia was part of the southern supercontinent, Gondwana. It was first identified in the form of a ninety-million-year-old pollen fossil.

The Wollemi pine is a truly unique tree and, when encountered, it is bound to conjure visions of dinosaurs striding through a Jurassic landscape. Its bark is covered in tightly knit nodules that are reminiscent of a well-known chocolate rice cereal. Branches emerge from the trunk as one single twig with fronds of thin, needlelike leaves growing in parallel along it. As the tree grows, it sends out fresh, bright green shoots that unfurl at the end of each branch, becoming a deep forest-green as they mature. The branches cover the tree from top to bottom, and male and female pine cones grow on the ends of the branches. The long, thin, yellow male cones store the pollen, while each round, spiky, green female cone holds hundreds of tiny, winged seeds. The tree is self-pollinating, but over the millennia it has relied primarily on the wind to distribute its seeds.

In 1994, David Noble, an avid canyoner and employee of the Australian national park service, was out looking for new canyoning sites. Looking down from the helicopter,

## AIR CORRESPONDENCE

Beginnings • Ancient Memory • Primeval Life

Noble spotted a small group of trees below that he didn't recognize and decided to take a closer look. By rappelling down the canyon, he reached the unidentified trees and, over the course of several visits, discovered that they were the ancient Wollemi pine. The largest specimen, at almost 130 feet (40 m) tall, has been named King Billy. The Wollemi pine is not to be confused with the King William pine (*Athrotaxis selaginoides*), which only grows in Tasmania and is a different species.

The exact site of the remaining Wollemi pines growing in the wild is a closely guarded secret. When the pines were first discovered, people visiting the trees brought pathogens with them on their shoes, and it quickly became apparent that the Wollemi pine is very susceptible to root rot (*Phytophthora cinnamomi*). Specialists used fungicide to treat the trees and the area was closed to unauthorized visitors.

With fewer than one hundred Wollemi pines left in the Wollemi National Park, and only around half of them mature trees, the tree is classified as critically endangered. On the red list of the International Union for Conservation of Nature (IUCN), it is legally protected in Australia through its designation as an Asset of Intergenerational Significance (AIS). The Wollemi pine was the first species to be covered by an AIS, which is designed to mitigate a potential zero-extinction event, empowering the national park to focus its resources and attention on this special tree.

*The Wollemi pine is a truly unique tree, and when encountered it is bound to conjure visions of dinosaurs striding through a Jurassic landscape.*

Despite this protection, the Wollemi pine still faces the threat of extinction from wildfires, the most recent of which was in 2020. Following the hottest and driest calendar year on record at that point, a fire started in the gorges of the Blue Mountains, threatening the Wollemi pine. In a previously unheard-of interagency response, air tankers, firefighters, and specialist teams were deployed to ensure the safety of the trees. Thanks to their efforts, the trees survived, and they continue to be protected through a close monitoring of weather conditions such as lightning storms and dry summers.

    The Royal Botanic Gardens in Sydney, Australia, became involved in attempting to preserve the tree and successfully cloned King Billy. This specimen can be found growing in the gardens today. The Wollemi pine also lives on across the world, as specimens are planted by various botanists and plant enthusiasts. This remains the best way to see these ancient beings, allowing them to thrive in the wild without disturbance, while honoring them in our gardens and arboreta.

> Look to the Wollemi pine for endurance.
>
> Affirmation

# PIPAL
*Ficus religiosa*

## *A sacred tree that guided Buddha to enlightenment*

The pipal tree, also known as the peepul, sacred fig, bo, or bodhi tree, is venerated by followers of Buddhism, Hinduism, Jainism, and Sikhism. Indigenous to Asia, the tree's unmistakable leaves appear in the Bronze Age art of the Indus Valley, an area covering Southern Asia. From here, thanks to the stories surrounding it and its religious significance, the pipal tree spread throughout the rest of Asia, and specimens can also be found across the continents.

The pipal tree begins life as an epiphyte high in the canopy of other trees. It initially grows without taking from the host tree, producing shoots and sending down roots in search of earth below. Once the roots reach the ground, they grow under the host tree and push up through it, splitting it in two. In this way, the pipal can also grow through bricks and sidewalks, reclaiming what is human-made. The leaf has no stalk, growing directly from the twigs and branches. The palm-sized leaves terminate in a thin, taillike tendril. These "tails" rustle in the breeze, creating the susurration for which the tree is known. The fruits are dark purple figs, although they do not grow from external flowers. Instead, the flowers are found within the fruit, meaning the fig wasp is the tree's main pollinator (see the Fig Tree, page 104, for further information).

The pipal tree has few medicinal properties, although juice from the leaves can alleviate earache, perhaps due to its antibacterial properties, and the bark, powdered and made into a paste, is helpful on wounds to treat infection.

It is the story of Buddha's enlightenment that brought the tree worldwide fame. Legend tells of how a young sixth-century BCE prince named Siddhartha Gautama became

## AIR CORRESPONDENCE

Enlightenment • Cosmic Power • Susurration

disillusioned by court life and the suffering in the world, so he set forth to find a solution. After six years of journeying, Gautama arrived in the village of Senanigama. Here, he rested under a pipal tree.

In the village, there lived a farmer's wife named Sujata. She dearly wanted a child and had been praying to the surrounding banyan trees in the hope they might grant her wish. When she saw the malnourished Gautama, she mistook him for a spirit of the trees and made him an offering of kheer, a traditional Indian dish of fragrant rice pudding. Gautama gratefully received the gift, which gave him the strength to continue his search for enlightenment.

He sat for seven days beneath a pipal tree, unblinking and staring into the tree. Within its branches he saw the Wheel of the World spinning, with the pipal at its center. On receiving this vision, he took the golden bowl that had contained the kheer and placed it in the nearby river, proclaiming that should the river take the bowl upstream, he would become Buddha. The river did so and Gautama became Buddha. The word *Buddha* means "the Enlightened or Awakened One," and statues and devotional books often show Buddha meditating beneath the pipal tree.

The tree under which Gautama became Buddha is thought to be the Bodh Gaya bodhi tree, located near the Mahabodhi Temple, a towering edifice that, in 2002, became a UNESCO World Heritage Site. It stands approximately 9 miles (14 km) from Gaya in the state of Bihar, East India, and has been a site of worship and pilgrimage since at least the third century BCE. The pipal tree at Gaya has been destroyed on numerous occasions over the centuries, but the monks living there have always planted new shoots in its place because the tree regenerates easily.

*The Vedas, the Sanskrit text that holds the knowledge and rituals used by Hindus, say that the pipal is a tree of cosmic power and regeneration.*

In the third century BCE, around three hundred years after Buddha is said to have gained enlightenment, an Indian emperor named Ashoka (also Aśoka), who ruled the Mauryan Empire that covered most of Southern Asia, is said to have destroyed the tree in opposition to its religious significance. When it regenerated, he saw the error of his ways and built the first temple at the spot.

Another story says that his wife, Empress Tishyarakshita, thought the tree must be a woman and that Ashoka was having an affair because he spent so long there. In this story it was Tishyarakshita who ordered the tree to be destroyed. Either way, the tree still stands, perhaps not the original tree but still a testament to its resilience and importance to the Buddhist faith.

In the Hindu tradition, the pipal tree is the tree of Vishnu and Lakshmi, two of the principal deities in the religion, Vishnu being the supreme being and Lakshmi his consort. Together, they represent prosperity, transformation, fertility, and wealth. The tree is an important part of festivals, ceremonies, and personal ritual. Jaggery (palm sugar), turmeric, chana dal, and small amounts of water from the Ganges River are mixed into a bowl of water or milk and poured onto the roots of the tree while mantras are chanted to Vishnu. This is often performed during Shukla Paksha, the period of time between the full and new moon each month.

The wood from the tree is used to make sacred tools such as vessels for drinking soma, a ritual drink from the Vedic tradition, and traditional fire drills (a small handheld stick slotted into another stick that is turned quickly to generate heat) used to light temple fires. The Vedas, the Sanskrit text that holds the knowledge and rituals used by Hindus, say that the pipal is a tree of cosmic power and regeneration. The Puranas, which hold the lore and stories of the Hindu religion, tell of the pipal purifying the air and blessing all those who shelter beneath it.

> Look to the pipal tree for enlightenment.
>
> Affirmation

# ROWAN
*Sorbus aucuparia*

## *A steadfast tree that shields against evil forces*

The rowan is a tree revered for its powers of protection. It can grow in the most inhospitable places and will live for up to two hundred years, offering protection for many generations. You will find it growing on mountains, riverbanks, gorges, woods, housing developments, and in urban backyards. Through the ages we have kept the rowan close, looking on it with affection and naming it witty, quick-beam, witchwood, witchbane, care-tree, and sip sap, all nods to the way the tree grows and the magic it holds.

The tree has a smooth, silvery bark and will grow up to 164 feet (50 m), depending on the conditions. The leaves grow in up to eight, slightly offset pairs along the stem, ending with one leaf. They have a gently serrated edge, giving them a feather-like feel and look, and making them easily distinguishable from those of the ash tree *(Fraxinus excelsior)*. The flowers are a creamy froth of delicate, white petals, and in the fall, they turn to scarlet-red berries, a favorite with woodland and garden birds alike. Where the flower has faded away, the end of each berry holds a five-pointed star associated with the pentagram of the Wiccan tradition, a symbol of protection and magic that embodies the elements of Earth, Air, Fire, Water, and Spirit.

Rowan is popularly used as a talisman in transitional spaces, such as chimneys, thresholds, doorways, stables, and rafters, protecting the household from witches, fairies, and the evil eye.

A "flying rowan" is particularly auspicious and was prized as a staff for protection on long journeys. Flying rowans can be found growing high in the fells of northern Britain and Scandinavia. They are rowans that have seeded between a cleft in the rocks and grown out from the side of a precipice, making it look like they are flying high

# AIR CORRESPONDENCE
Ethereal Magic • Feathers • Flight

above the ground. This has given the tree the name "mountain ash."

Amulets are frequently made from rowan and carried in the pocket or worn as jewelry. In this way, rowan not only offers protection but is also said to add a year to the life of those who carry it. Rowan lore traveled with those immigrating to North America, particularly to Newfoundland and Nova Scotia in Canada. There are records of settlers planting rowans outside their homes, a popular way to protect the household, and in Nova Scotia, pigs with rowan collars and sprigs around their sties fattened quicker than others.

It is claimed that the Danes used rowan to protect their boats against Rán, a Norse goddess of the ocean who is said to net and drown hapless sailors. The idea that a boat made of rowan will protect the seagoer is played out in the Northumbrian (England) song, "The Laidley Worm of Spindleston Heugh." In this tale, the brother of a cursed princess returns to save her. The witch who has cast the curse sees the brother's ship approaching and tries to sink it with magic. It is here that the verse in the ballad notes:

*It is claimed that the Danes used rowan to protect their boats against Rán, a Norse goddess of the ocean who is said to net and drown hapless sailors.*

*The spells were vain. The hags returned*
*To the queen in sorrowful mood,*
*Crying that witches have no power,*
*Where there is rown-tree wood.*

In Norse lore, rowan is sometimes referred to as Thor's helper because in one of Thor's journeys to Jotunheim (the land of the giants), he crosses the raging torrent that is the River Vimur and uses a rowan tree to pull himself to safety.

The tree has further associations with the realms of giants in Irish lore, where we find a magical rowan tree in the Wood of Dubhros. This rowan tree was accidently seeded by a warrior band called the Men of Dea, who were returning from a competition with rival warriors, the Fianna. The berries had come from the Tuatha Dé Danaan (a supernatural race in Irish mythology), and the tree that grew from them offered everlasting health to those who ate them. The Tuatha Dé Danaan heard of the new tree and concluded that it must have come from their lands. They decided the tree must be protected. They gave the job to Searbhán Lochlannach (the Surly One of Lochlann), a giant of a man who was eventually killed by Diarmuid of the Fianna when seeking the berries for his lover, Gráinne.

Although rowan is mostly relied on for protection, it also has some medicinal and nutritional value. The bark can be used as a cure for diarrhea; however, the berries, if eaten raw, contain parasorbic acid, which not only tastes bitter but can also cause nausea and indigestion. The acid can be removed through boiling, and a popular way to eat rowan berries is in a jam or jelly as an accompaniment to meat and cheese. Traditional recipes suggest boiling rowan berries with crab apples, straining them, and adding sugar and lemon juice before boiling again until they reach the required temperature to make jam. The high vitamin C content means they have been useful in the past for sailors fending off scurvy and as a gargle to soothe a sore throat.

The wood was often used for the handles of tools, plows, bowls, and cups; as a way of protecting the crops while they were harvested; and to protect food during preparation. It was said that the milk would likely curdle if the handle of the butter churn was not made of rowan, while the pins that secured the yokes to the oxen plowing the fields were said to protect the cattle and crops if made from rowan wood.

## Look to the rowan for protection.

Affirmation

Chapter 4

# EARTH: TREES OF LIFE

Trees have long been a source of food for all life on the planet. Their roots hold the soil and prevent valuable nutrients from running off into rivers. Their bark, leaves, and fruit provide us with medicine and sustenance. Mother Earth runs through their xylem and phloem to the food we eat, keeping us grounded and growing strong. Earth is synonymous with the womb, a life-giver, bringer of the harvest, and protector. In trees of the Earth, we find food for our tables, the foundations of cities, immortal life, weapons and tools, medicine, and complex ecosystems.

# OLIVE
*Olea europaea*

## *A hardy tree that speaks of peace, strength, and longevity*

The olive is an ancient tree typically associated with the Mediterranean, in particular Italy and Greece, though cultivated varieties grow worldwide. Olive tree fossils thought to be fifty to sixty thousand years old have been unearthed on the Greek island of Santorini in the Aegean Sea, and charred remains of olive stones have been found in Egyptian tombs dating to the Thirteenth Dynasty (ca. 1803–1649 BCE). The European olive (*Olea europaea*) is a cultivated species that is only propagated by grafting it to a specimen of wild olive (*O. europaea* subsp. *europaea*), a reminder of our dependence on the gifts Earth grants us.

The olive tree is a hardy and drought-resistant evergreen that can produce crops for thousands of years. The trunk is often twisted and gnarled with age, bent by the wind and the often inhospitable climate in which the tree thrives. Slender, yet tough, leaves appear to grow haphazardly, and their silvery undersides offer a glimpse of the olive's softer side. Tiny, white, four-petaled flowers produce small fruits, ripening from green to black and providing a glut suitable for harvest every two years in the fall. The oldest olive tree in the world is thought to be the Olive Tree of Vouves in the village of Ano Vouves in Crete. Between two and four thousand years old, it still produces olives.

The rich, brown, swirling tones of olive wood, when worked, make it sought after for ornamental items. The fruit is enjoyed across the globe, with just over 3 million tons (2.7 million t) consumed each year. If not made into oil, olives are typically soaked in brine to draw out the bitterness of the fruits when picked fresh from the tree. They are rich in oleic acid, vitamins, and minerals, and they contain antioxidants, which have been found to help combat inflammation and reduce the risk of heart disease.

## EARTH CORRESPONDENCE

Mountains • Salt • Abundance

In ancient Egyptian, Greek, and Roman cultures, olive oil was used to anoint kings and the dead, consecrate sacred tools and objects, and fuel small, traditional terra-cotta oil lamps for lighting homes and temples.

> *In the Greek myth of Theseus, . . . he gives an offering of an olive branch to Apollo so he may be successful in slaying the Minotaur.*

In general, the olive tree is a symbol of prosperity, peace, strength, and longevity. Passing an olive branch to someone is a sign of peace or a truce, while farmers once burned an olive branch as an offering to the gods to ensure a good harvest. A sprig of olive worn by a bride indicates her chastity, and olive trees were often planted next to sarcophagi as a symbol of eternal life.

In ancient Greece, those olive trees that were considered sacred and the subject of myth were called *moriai*. This signified that they belonged to the state. Perhaps one of the most famous of these can be found growing at the temple of Erechtheion at the Acropolis in Athens, Greece. The myth associated with the tree tells how Athena (Greek goddess of war strategy, creativity, and wisdom) and Poseidon (ruler of the seas and brother of Zeus) both wanted to offer their protection to Athens, then known as the city of Aktaio. Neither wanted to share custodianship of the city, and so Poseidon challenged Athena to a competition. Each of them would give the city a gift. Whichever gift the people preferred, the giver of that gift would rule over the city.

Poseidon gave his gift by striking a stone from which sprung forth a fountain of salt water. Athena struck the earth, and from it grew an olive tree. The people of Aktaio had no desire for salt water, but the olive tree was a bountiful gift indeed. And so it was that Athena became the guardian of Aktaio and the city became Athens, renamed in her honor.

In 480 BCE, during the Greco-Persian Wars, Persian forces led by Xerxes the Great conquered the city and ordered it to be torched. The day after the city was sacked, Athena's olive tree grew new roots, which gave the Athenians hope. The tree stands witness to this day, and the Acropolis receives around three million visitors every year.

In the Greek myth of Theseus, hero and prince of Athens, he gives an offering of an olive branch to Apollo so he may be successful in slaying the Minotaur. Myth also records that Heracles (also Hercules), famed for his completion of the twelve labors set by King Eurystheus, succeeded in his first labor of killing the Nemean Lion thanks to a club made of olive wood. Olive branches and wreaths were frequently associated with Zeus, and olive wreaths, as well as laurel wreaths, were also presented to Olympian winners.

In the Christian Bible, the Book of Genesis, which tells the story of Noah and the Great Flood, describes how the olive branch is brought to Noah by a dove as a sign that the waters are receding. The Bible also tells of how Jesus is said to have retired to the Mount of Olives, a mountain ridge with olive groves on the east side of Jerusalem, in order to seek peace before his crucifixion. In Islam, the olive tree is sometimes seen as the world tree and the embodiment of the prophet Muhammad. It is said that on each leaf, one of the ninety-nine names of God is written.

## Look to the olive tree for peace in times of conflict.

Affirmation

# FIG
*Ficus carica*

## *A spiritual tree of abundance and fertility*

The fig tree (*Ficus carica*) was one of the first plants cultivated by humans. We know this because fossils dating to the Neolithic Period have been found in an archaeological site in the Jordan Valley, known as Gigal I. Within the site, there is also evidence of arable crops, which indicates early farming in this area. The fig tree needs sun and free-draining soil to thrive, and the fruit can be eaten fresh or dried.

Fig trees grow best in Turkey, Egypt, Morocco, and Algeria, and it is these countries that provide the world with over half the figs for the dinner table. There is one fig that will tolerate colder, drier climates. These figs, commonly known as the rock fig (*Ficus petiolaris*), are endemic to Mexico.

The fig tree has large, distinctive, handlike leaves with three to five rounded lobes. Fruit buds form in the cleft of the leaf stems where they meet with the branches and swell until they form a deep purple to brown fruit. There are up to 750 tiny seeds within the sweet, deep red flesh of the fruit.

As with all trees in the fig family (Moraceae), the main pollinator for the species is the fig wasp (*Blastophaga psenes*). This is because the flower grows inside the fruit rather than the fruit forming behind the external flower. To overcome the obvious pollination barriers an internal flower presents, the flower inside the fruit emits a scent that attracts the fig wasp. Female fig wasps lay their eggs in the fig and, in turn, the fig produces food for the larvae when they emerge.

It is then that the male wasps fertilize the female larvae and create holes in the fig for the females to escape from once they are grown. The fully formed female wasps emerge covered in fig pollen and the process starts again, with the female wasp carrying the pollen to another fig tree and to the flower at the fruit's heart.

## EARTH CORRESPONDENCE
Fertility • The First Garden • Femininity

The milky sap produced by fig branches can be a skin irritant and can increase skin's sensitivity to sun, but has been used to treat warts in the past. The English herbalist John Gerard noted in *Gerard's Herball, or Generall Historie of Plantes* (1597) that a paste of figs could be used to reduce swelling and that figs and honey were good for a sore throat. When mixed together as a gargle with hyssop (*Hyssopus officinalis*) and rue (*Ruta graveolens*), figs proved effective for coughs, and Gerard even proffered figs mashed with rue and walnut kernels as an antidote to the bubonic plague that occurred during the sixteenth century, a second wave of the disease known as the Black Death.

*In Italy it is said that you should not fall asleep beneath a fig tree for fear of meeting the women who dwell within them.*

In Greek mythology, Syke, one of the eight dryad nymphs who live in the trees, is said to preside over the fig tree. This has led to fig trees being associated with the otherworlds, and in Italy it is said that you should not fall asleep beneath one for fear of meeting the women who dwell within them.

In Britain, there is anecdotal evidence that stewed, strained, and spiced figs were added to ale as a Good Friday drink and that in North Buckinghamshire, England, figs were eaten on Palm Sunday. However, in the Bible, Jesus curses the fig tree because he is hungry and the fig tree's fruits are not yet ripe. The next day, the disciples of Jesus note that the fig has withered and died, and so Jesus tells them this is a sign that God is always listening and will grant their prayers.

The fig tree is sometimes said to be the original Tree of Knowledge from the Garden of Eden in the Book of Genesis. In fact, many images of Adam and Eve depict them holding fig leaves to cover themselves when they see that they are naked.

A story from Watford, England, tells of a priest who could not convert a member of the community. The person he was trying to convert asked that, when they died and were interred, a fig be placed in their hand so that, should God and heaven exist, a fig tree would grow from their grave. This came to pass, and the fig tree grew on the grave until around 1960. In this way, the fig seems to walk a line between being a sacred and a cursed tree.

In Italy, the fig tree is the inspiration for a hand gesture considered vulgar and obscene. The *mano in fica* involves balling your fist, placing your thumb between your first and middle fingers, and pointing it at the person you wish to insult. The expression dates from the Roman era and later became an amulet known as the *higa hispánica* during the Italian Renaissance. The amulets are miniature versions of a forearm and fisted hand with the thumb between the first two fingers. In this form, it protects against the evil eye. Both the fruit of the fig tree and this gesture are meant to represent female sexuality, in particular a woman's vulva, and the tree more generally is considered a symbol of fertility and femininity.

> Look to the fig tree for feminine power.
>
> ———
> Affirmation

# WILD APPLE
*Malus sylvestris*

## *A tree associated with love, myth, and healing*

The wild apple, more commonly known as the crab apple, is the original species from which the domestic apple was cultivated. Crab apples can live for a hundred years and are short, shrub-like trees with an irregular shape. If planted in exposed areas, the trunks and branches can become gnarled and twisted by the elements. Oval leaves end with a small point, and white to pink blossoms appear in spring, followed by marble-sized, chartreuse-green and golden yellow apples.

The name is thought to come from the Old English *crabbe*, meaning "bitter taste," and Henry David Thoreau, a nineteenth-century American writer, is quoted as describing the taste as, "sour enough to set a squirrel's teeth on edge and make a jay scream." This might explain why it is known as grindstone apple in Wiltshire in England, referring to the sharpening of reaping hooks with the fruit's acidic juice.

In North America, John Chapman, born in 1774 in Massachusetts and a leading grower, is inextricably linked with the apple. He believed in growing domestic apples from seed, not grafting them, and became an apple-seed-planting nomad, introducing seed-grown apple orchards to the US states of Pennsylvania, Ohio, Indiana, Illinois, and West Virginia, as well as the Canadian province of Ontario. He was considered a conservation pioneer, and as he traveled, he planted community nurseries and left them in the charge of a local who sold shares in the orchards on his behalf. Many of the apples from these orchards were used to make cider and applejack (a brandy distilled from cider).

Chapman's endeavors were not entirely altruistic, however, as the presence of trees at boundaries was crucial when asserting a claim to territory and in the American frontier.

## EARTH CORRESPONDENCE

Health • Blessings • Consequences

This meant that he owned over a 1,000 acres (400 hectares), which he eventually sold. There is no doubt, though, that Chapman (or Johnny Appleseed, as he became known) was responsible for the spread of the apple orchard in the Midwest and parts of Canada.

The apple in myth and story is closely linked to health, fertility, and immortality. Often these apples are gold, perhaps suggesting they are the wild apple rather than domestic varieties. In *The Arabian Nights*, a magic apple from Samarkand is said to have the power to cure all human diseases. In Greek and Norse mythologies, apples hold life-giving properties and are associated with the gods.

The Greeks believed that immortality and youth lay at the heart of a golden apple guarded by the Hesperides (nymphs of the sunset) in the Garden of the Hesperides. The apples were retrieved by Heracles (Hercules) in the eleventh of his labors. In the "Judgment of Paris" myth, the apple is weaponized by Eris, goddess of discord, who, when she is not invited to the wedding of Peleus and Thetis, crashes the party, throwing a golden apple onto the bride and groom's table and claiming that the most beautiful goddess should win the apple. Zeus is to decide the winner. Hera, Athena, and Aphrodite are the front-runners. Zeus, showing his usual reluctance to court trouble, decides that a mortal, the Trojan prince Paris, should judge the competition instead. The goddesses try to bribe Paris for his vote. Paris chooses Aphrodite because she promises him the most handsome woman in the world. He goes on to meet Helen of Sparta, who falls in love with him, and they run away together, sparking the Trojan War.

*In* The Arabian Nights, *a magic apple from Samarkand is said to have the power to cure all human diseases.*

In Norse mythology, the gods enjoy immortality thanks to the golden apples in the goddess Idun's orchard, which they must eat to maintain their youth. In the "Theft of Idun's Apples," the trickster god Loki gives Idun and her apples to a giant in exchange for his life. The gods start to age, and Loki is sent to retrieve the apples, or the gods will die. This story features one of the most famous showdowns between the gods of Asgard and the frost giants of Jotunheim.

*Malus*, the genus assigned to the apple family (Rosaceae), is Latin for "evil," which the apple sometimes appears to be. Indeed, it is an apple eaten in the Garden of Eden by Adam and Eve that makes them aware of their nakedness and, in turn, ashamed. Disney's movie *Snow White* sees the lead character falling foul of the apple when her stepmother, disguised as a hag, gifts her a poisoned fruit. However, in both cases, the apple is a passive bystander, perhaps representing that the power within it depends on the desires of the person who wields it.

For hundreds of years, the apple has been used in folk medicine. With honey it becomes a prophylaxis for those with heart conditions. In the Nine Herb Charm, a narrative charm within the *Lacnunga*, a tenth-century Anglo-Saxon healing text, the crab apple guards against snake venom. Figuratively, this could be because the hard apple will pull out the snake's teeth on biting it, or perhaps because the bitter taste would drive it away. It is well known that the apple is rich in vitamins and nutrients. Anecdotal evidence suggests that apple cider vinegar can be used as a tonic for cleansing and purging, thanks to its anti-inflammatory properties. It can also be made into crab apple jelly, cider, wine, and, in medieval times, verjuice (sour juice).

Blessing the orchard, a tradition known as wassailing, has seen a huge revival in many UK villages. The name is thought to derive from the Old English phrase *waes hael*, meaning "good health." In an orchard wassail, the community gathers to make a "hullabaloo" in order to wake the trees and frighten away evil spirits. Sometimes shotguns are fired into the trees and songs are sung so the village may have a good crop of apples in the fall.

# Look to the apple tree for perpetuity in your actions.

Affirmation

# YOSHINO CHERRY
*Prunus* × *yedoensis*

## *A tree of transient beauty and cultural significance*

The Yoshino cherry was grown in Japan as a hybrid cherry tree, embodying the beauty of both the Oshima cherry (*Prunus speciosa*) and the Japanese wild cherry (*Prunus itosakura*, also known as *Edo higan*). It is one of the most popular cultivated cherry trees in the world.

Also known as the Somei-Yoshino, the tree is relatively young, with the oldest known specimen standing in Kaiseizan Park, in Koriyama, Japan, and just under 150 years old. The tree was given the name Somei-Yoshino in 1900, derived from the place in which it was cultivated, Somei village (Toshima, a municipality of Tokyo) and Mount Yoshino, where the Japanese mountain cherry (*Prunus jamasakura*) grows.

The striking white flowers of the Oshima cherry, combined with the umbrella canopy of the wild cherry and its habit of blooming before producing leaves, result in a medium-height tree that grows quickly and provides a dramatic show in spring. The almond-scented blossom with gold stamens is white to pale pink, contrasting perfectly against the smooth, dark gray bark of the trunk. Flowering from early to mid-spring, the tree can be found in parks and cities across Japan, as well as along riverbanks and footpaths—a sign of spring and hope for the Japanese people.

The blossom of the cherry is called *sakura* in Japanese—*sa* refers to the deity of the rice plant, and *kura* denotes the divine seat of a deity. This links the cherry tree to the rice harvest, as the blossom precedes the harvest. Inari, goddess of the rice harvest, is often pictured with cherry blossom in her hair.

The cherry blossom is Japan's national flower and appears on the silver yen (100-yen coin). Its flowers represent the fleeting nature of life, known as *mono no aware*, or "the pathos of things," and is the ultimate

## EARTH CORRESPONDENCE

Life Cycles • Hope • Peace

reminder of the beauty and transience of all life. The cherry blossom season is of such cultural importance that the Japanese meteorological office tracks the blooming of the trees each year. So popular is the Yoshino cherry that it has become a celebrity tree in its own right.

Cherry blossom parties, known as *hanami*, involve feasting, picnicking beneath the trees, and taking walks under the canopies of blossoms. This celebration has its roots in eighth-century China, where the tradition was enjoyed by aristocrats. *Hanami* means "watching blossom" or "flower watching" and is a time for contemplation as well as celebration. Night gatherings are called *yozakura*, and illuminations, food stalls, and up-lit cherry trees allow the festival to carry on into the night. In Tokyo alone, there are over a thousand cherry trees, many of them illuminated at night for those gathering to celebrate.

The blossom lasts for two weeks, and its beauty and transient nature have long been a constant source of inspiration for artists, writers, and poets. "Sakura, Sakura," often sung by preschoolers, is a folk song that has been popular in Japanese schools since the late 1800s. The song celebrates the cherry blossom and sings of its ethereal nature and the tradition of flower watching.

Tokyo gifted three thousand cherry trees to Washington, DC, in 1912 as a symbol of friendship. To commemorate this gift, a four-week National Cherry Blossom Festival is held in Washington, DC, from early to mid-spring. Music, dance, parades, parties, food, family fun, and shows celebrating Japanese culture all make up this celebration of spring.

The cherry tree appears in the stories and lore of Japan and is most famously associated with the goddess Konohanasakuya-hime, who is sometimes known as Sakura-hime. Her name translates as "Blossom Princess," and she symbolizes the cherry tree. As the goddess of volcanoes, Konohanasakuya-hime is also the goddess of Mount Fuji, an active volcano on the Japanese island of Honshu. Shinto shrines have been built on the slopes of Mount Fuji to honor Konohanasakuya-hime, since it is believed she will prevent the volcano from erupting. Stories tell of how the goddess destroyed the Yatsugatake Mountains adjacent to Mount Fuji because she wanted no mountains to be higher than her own.

A popular Japanese folk tale tells of how, during a smallpox epidemic in the eleventh century, a young boy sought a cure for his mother. A vision showed him that he should go to a stream on the slopes of Mount Fuji in search of this cure. He did this, and a woman in white appeared to him and guided him to healing waters. The waters cured his mother, and the woman told him he should return as many times as was needed to cure the whole village. He did so, enduring repeated journeys in order to cure his community.

When he had finished his task, he returned to the river to thank the woman, only to discover that the river had dried up, and he watched as the woman ascended on clouds into the sky. Only then did he realize that it was Konohanasakuya-hime who had helped him.

So strong is the image of Konohanasakuya-hime and the cherry tree that she has become the subject of a manga series (a style of cartoon/graphic novel unique to Japan) by Arina Tanemura titled *Sakura Hime: The Legend of Princess Sakura*. The story follows a fourteen-year-old princess who wants to marry for love, her epic adventures to find it, and her refusal to settle for anything less.

# Look to the cherry tree for a reminder of the cycles in life.

---

Affirmation

# KOA
*Acacia koa*

## A supportive tree of spiritual and practical value

The koa tree is found on the Hawaiian islands of Hawaiʻi, Molokaʻi, Maui, Oʻahu, and Kauaʻi. It is a member of the legume, pea, and bean family (Fabaceae), and its name is derived from the Hawaiian word for "warrior." A tree of strength, it is also known as ironwood and has found a place not only at the heart of Hawaiian culture but also at the heart of the islands' ecosystems.

Koa thrives in soil rich in volcanic ash and can reach a height of over 100 feet (30 m) in these conditions. The tree starts its life with fernlike fronds known as bipinnate compound leaves. As the tree ages, the leaves become single, sickle-shaped leaves known as phyllodes. These are modified leaves that allow sunlight through the tree canopy to the lower branches of the tree and the forest floor.

The koa tree's flowers form yellow clusters with hundreds of stamens, and the tree can flower all year-round in some areas. The fruit is similar to a pea pod, turning brown/black and containing up to twelve seeds. The seeds have a tough coating, making them resilient to adverse environmental factors such as heavy rain. This means the seed can remain dormant for up to twenty-five years if the coating is not broken down, either by the elements or when eaten and processed by animals.

The koa is a fast-growing tree and, as with many plants in the Fabaceae family, it is important for putting nitrogen back into the soil, creating fertile ground for the understory.

The koa tree is also excellent at supporting the water cycle of the forest. Its canopy collects water from the clouds and fog, and the dense foliage slows heavy rainfall, preventing torrents of water from causing soil runoff. The roots also run deep, holding the soil together, and again preventing damage from adverse weather.

## EARTH CORRESPONDENCE
Strength • Ancestors • Ecosystems

*The koa is central to the stories of ancient warriors and acts as an ancestor tree for the Hawaiian people. It is a link to those who have walked the Earth before them and the current generation.*

When felled, the trunk is a reddish brown and is sought after for its aesthetically pleasing finish when polished. Its most well-known use is as dugout canoes called *wa'a*. King Kamehameha the Great is said to have created wa'a and weapons from the wood of the koa tree. During his reign, this wood was readily available on Hawai'i, which is also known as the Big Island. The weapons made from the tree were called *lei-o-mano*. Carved into a bat or paddle-like shape, the edge of the broad blade was studded with lethally sharp shark teeth and marlin bills.

King Kamehameha traveled in wa'a with his warriors to unite the islands of Hawai'i. In this way, the tree became synonymous with warriors, the Hawaiian word for which is *koa*. For a long time, the wood was considered so sacred that it could only be used by royalty, but when Kamehameha died in 1819, his wife lifted this restriction and koa wood became available to all.

From this point on, koa wood was used for food bowls called *umeke*. Knives for domestic use, called *niho* or *oki*, a little like modern craft knives, were created from koa wood and shark teeth. Boats for fishing and traveling continued to be made from the wood of the koa tree, and the first surfboards were made from koa wood thanks to its durability and water-resistant qualities.

Hawaiian *pahu*, meaning "drum," are created from a single log with shark or ray skin stretched over the top. The drums are usually made from the coconut tree (*Cocos nucifera*), but koa wood has also been used for these instruments. An example of a drum made from koa and sharkskin is held in the Smithsonian National Museum of Natural History in Washington, DC.

Instruments made of koa wood have a distinctive sound, and the first settlers in Hawai'i used it for ukeleles. Guitars made of koa wood have remained popular, and the American electric guitar company Fender has created an artisan range of Stratocasters that uses highly polished koa wood.

Koa has entered every aspect of the Hawaiian home through furniture, kitchenware, canoes, surfboards, and instruments, and if used sustainably, it is said to represent mālama 'āina, the concept of caring for the land.

The koa tree not only supports human endeavors but also provides an important ecosystem for several species. It is the preferred tree for two endemic butterfly species: the green Hawaiian blue (*Udara blackburni*) and the Kamehameha butterfly (*Vanessa tameamea*). The caterpillars of the green Hawaiian blue enjoy the fruits and flowers, while the sap is eaten by the adult Kamehameha butterfly. The Kamehameha butterfly, known as the *pulelehua* in Hawaiian, has deep orangey-red and black markings and in 2009 was named the state insect of Hawai'i.

Another insect reliant on the koa tree is the koa bug (*Coleotichus blackburniae*). A brightly colored shield bug, it uses an elongated snout to push into the seeds of the tree and harvest the contents. Several species of the Hawaiian honeycreeper bird also feed and nest within the koa tree, including the endangered 'akiapōlā'au (*Hemignathus wilsoni*), the Hawaiian 'i'iwi (*Drepanis coccinea*), and the 'apapane (*Himatione sanguinea*).

The koa is central to the stories of ancient warriors and acts as an ancestor tree for the Hawaiian people. It is a link to those who have walked the Earth before them and the current generation. In this way, it is a venerated tree. Years of forestry, logging, and cattle rearing have meant that Hawai'i's koa trees have suffered heavy losses. Thankfully, there is work being done to reestablish the trees and turn grassland used for cattle back into koa forests so this tree can continue to support future generations.

## Look to the koa for the spirit of the warrior.

Affirmation

# CINCHONA
*Cinchona officinalis*

## *A historically and culturally important tree offering healing*

The cinchona tree is found in the tropical Andean cloud forests of Ecuador and Peru, one of the world's most unique and biodiverse habitats and home to many medicinal plants and specimens crucial to human health. Famous for providing European colonists with a cure for malaria, the cinchona tree was at the center of trade between Europe and South America for almost three centuries.

The cinchona is a relatively small, shrub-like tree, growing to around 33 feet (10 m), with cracked, rusty red bark. Its evergreen leaves are oval and pointed at both ends. The tubular flowers, the lobes of which have tiny hairs on the edges, are white with pink to red centers and have a pleasing scent. Multiple clusters of brown capsules containing up to fifty samaras (winged seeds) are produced.

Quinine, one of the alkaloids within the bark, is the reason for the tree's fame and is credited with the success of European colonizers not only in South America but also Africa and Asia. To recognize its significance, we need to go back to the Roman Empire. Malaria is Italian for "bad air"—*mal aria*—and there is evidence that malaria epidemics ravaged Roman populations as far back as the fifth century CE.

A theory proffered by American archaeologist David Soren argues that malaria played a part in the final fall of the Roman Empire. In 2003, following the excavation of a cemetery in Umbria, Italy, Soren and a team of archaeologists from the University of Arizona found DNA evidence that this might be true. If they'd had the cinchona tree, perhaps Rome would not have fallen.

Quinine acts as an antipyretic—when Spanish colonists arrived in South America, bringing malaria with them, the Quechua, Cañari, and Chimú of Peru, Bolivia, and Ecuador shared the tree's cure with them. The Indigenous

## EARTH CORRESPONDENCE
Healing · Abundance · Wealth

peoples of South America, sometimes referred to as the Quechua people after the group of languages they speak, call cinchona bark *quinquina*, meaning "bark of barks." It was these peoples who showed the Jesuit missionaries arriving in the early 1600s how to use the bark to treat fevers. Once the Jesuits realized the bark could treat malaria, they established trade routes to transport it to Europe. It became known as Jesuit's Powder and Jesuit Bark, but it was always the Quechua people's knowledge that saved the lives of so many Europeans.

Throughout the sixteenth and seventeenth centuries, there are records of various Spanish, Italian, and British physicians using cinchona bark to cure fevers. One account explains why the tree is called cinchona. The story goes that the wife of the 4th Count of Chinchón (Spanish Viceroy of Peru), Francisca Henriques de Ribera, became ill with tertian fever while in Lima in 1630.

She was given a traditional remedy, thought to be the bark of the *quinquina* tree, and made a full recovery. When Carl Linnaeus, an eighteenth-century Swedish biologist, heard this story, he named the tree after the countess. The story was recorded in 1663 by Italian physician Sebastiano Bado, who heard it from a Peruvian merchant, but it is considered more legend than fact.

Further records show that English physician Robert Talbor administered an effective fever remedy to King Charles II of England and the son of Louis XIV of France. The components of this cure were kept secret and called *Água de Inglaterra* (Water from England). When the ingredients were divulged, they were found to contain rose leaves, lemon juice, cinchona bark, and wine. The wine was included not only to make the bitter bark taste better but also because the alcohol dissolved the bark's vital alkaloids much better than water.

By the 1800s, "fever tree" plantations were well established in Dutch Indonesia, French Algeria, and British India. Hybrid trees were propagated, and the quinine was used to treat the scourge of the British Army: malaria. During this time, like the cure given to Charles II, soldiers are said to have mixed the ground-up bark with gin, rum, brandy, and arrack (a distilled alcoholic drink), making it more palatable and effective. According to a BBC article, "The Tree That Changed the World" (2021), between 1848 and 1861, Britain spent around £6.4 million a year importing cinchona bark.

Eventually, malaria mutated and became more resistant to the bark cures. In some cases, the quinine from the cinchona was replaced by the more readily available sweet wormwood (*Artemisia annua*). In time, the drugs used to treat fevers could be made artificially, and so the tree became less valuable. However, as a result of overharvesting in the 1800s and destructive harvesting methods, regeneration has proved difficult for a tree that produces many seeds but has a very low success rate for germination due to the size of the seed. Records from 1805 by explorers show that there were once 25,000 cinchona trees in the Ecuadorean Andes. Now, the Podocarpus National Park of Ecuador holds just twenty-nine specimens.

Today, the cinchona tree is the national tree of both Peru and Ecuador, and is found on Peru's coat of arms along with the vicuña, a wild Peruvian member of the camel family. There are twenty species of *Cinchona* in Peru, growing in Cutervo National Park, Manú National Park, and Semilla Bendita Botanical Gardens. Manú National Park is a UNESCO Biosphere Reserve and remains largely untouched by humans.

There is hope for the cinchona tree. In 2021, a group called Jardín Etnobotánico - Semilla Bendita (the latter meaning "blessed seeds"), based in Peru, planted 2,021 seeds for the bicentennial anniversary of the country's independence. The group continues to champion the cinchona, working to conserve this very special tree.

## Look to the cinchona tree for the hidden treasures in life.

Affirmation

# KAURI PINE
*Agathis australis*

*Provider of rich resources, the kauri is a long-lived and sacred tree*

Cousin to the Wollemi pine (*Wollemia nobilis*; see page 86) and the monkey puzzle tree (*Araucaria araucana*), the kauri pine is an ancient tree from the conifer group. It is found on New Zealand's North Island (*Te Ika-a-Māui*), in Waipoua Forest, the Waitākere and Hunua Ranges, and on the Great Barrier Island.

Known as a giant of the New Zealand boreal forests, kauri pine can reach heights of 130 feet (40 m) and live for over a thousand years, its trunk attaining a diameter of 6½ to 13 feet (2–4 m). So iconic is the kauri pine that if even only a few exist in a forest, this becomes known as a kauri forest.

The kauri pine shares the emergent layer of the forest canopy with other trees in the conifer group such as the tōtara (*Podocarpus totara*), rimu (*Dacrydium cupressinum*), rewarewa (*Knightia excelsa*), and pōhutukawa (*Metrosideros excelsa*). The largest known kauri tree specimen still in existence is called Tāne Mahuta, after the Māori god of the forests and birds. Tāne Mahuta is thought to be between 1,500 and 2,000 years old and has a diameter of around 13 feet (4 m).

In adolescence, the tree's canopy is conical and the trunk straight. As the trees age, the trunks swell and the canopy splays, offering a home for a plethora of wildlife. "Kauri" is the Māori name for the tree and refers to the copper-colored underlayer that is revealed when the smooth bark of the trunk cracks. The flaking of the bark provides a defense against parasites, and the resin produced by the tree is antibacterial and antifungal, allowing it to heal trunk injuries. As the tree grows, it drops the lower branches to prevent vines from taking hold from below. However, there are often many epiphytes, such as ferns and orchids, growing in the crooks of the upper branches.

## EARTH CORRESPONDENCE
Nourishment • Strong Foundations • Guardianship

The kauri is an evergreen and produces pinnate leaves that grow in pairs, terminating with one single leaf at the end of the twig. It has distinctive cones: The female cones are round, and the male cones are oval-shaped. It is a keystone species, able to create its own ecosystem by producing podzol, a type of soil found in coniferous forests. As the trees drop their leaves, the organic matter breaks down to create a thick layer of nutrient-rich soil, often above a layer of sand or otherwise infertile soil.

The acidic soil in kauri forests means that a number of rare species are only found in these habitats. For example, in the understory of the kauri forest, kauri grass (*Astelia trinervia*) and an orchid called kauri greenhood (*Pterostylis agathicola*) can be found. Birds such as the ruru/morepork (*Ninox novaeseelandiae*), kōtare/sacred kingfisher (*Todiramphus sanctus*), pīwakawaka/New Zealand fantail (*Rhipidura fuliginosa*), kūkupa/kererū/New Zealand wood pigeon (*Hemiphaga novaeseelandiae*), shining cuckoo (*Chalcites lucidus*), and the endangered kiwi (*Apteryx species*) also all make their homes in the kauri forest and play a part in the unique soundscape found there. Another unique aspect of podzol is the mycorrhizal fungi in the soil and roots of the kauri tree. The fungi and the tree have a symbiotic relationship that is vital to maintaining the balance and health of the ecosystem in these forests.

*The largest known kauri tree specimen still in existence is called Tāne Mahuta, after the Māori god of the forests and birds.*

Over the centuries, the Māori have used the tree in a variety of ways, such as for boats and houses. The waxy resin produced by the bark makes excellent kindling for fires and serves as a chewing gum for oral hygiene. When burned down to a black powder and mixed with animal fat, the resin creates a black-blue ink that can be used for tattoos.

In the 1300s, many kauri trees were cleared by Māori for sweet potato farming when they arrived in New Zealand from Polynesia. Later, European settlers discovered that the adolescent trees made ideal masts for ships. A layer of resin was also unearthed in the ground where old trees once stood, and it was soon found to be a rich resource that could be used in varnishes. Soon, thousands of settlers, known as gum diggers, were paying for licenses to dig for the resin and transport it back to Europe.

When the ground supply ran out, the trees were tapped for resin using brutal, non-sustainable methods, and the kauri forests suffered many losses. In 1952, the kauri was finally given protection in the Waipoua Forest Sanctuary, and since 1987, the kauri trees of New Zealand have been protected by the Department of Conservation.

The kauri tree features in the stories and mythology of the Māori people. It is said that in the beginning, Tohorā (whale) and Tiwaiwaka (the kauri tree) both lived on land. They were great friends, but Tohorā wanted to live in the ocean and Tiwaiwaka did not wish to leave the land. So the two exchanged skins, which meant they would forever be in each other's company. As a result, the kauri has scaly bark and the whale has smooth skin.

In one Māori creation myth, Tāne Mahuta, the *atua* (power, spirit, or god) of the forest, is revered as the son of the sky mother, Ranginui (Rangi), and the earth father, Papatūānuku (Papa). Rangi and Papa were once joined together, but this meant that the world was in darkness. Tāne Mahuta was frustrated by the eternal darkness and stood between his parents, pushing them asunder. He remains as the kauri tree, a guardian god holding the earth and the sky apart.

For the Māori, all humans and nonhumans are siblings: children of Tāne Mahuta. The kauri tree is *taonga*, a word that means "treasure," and a ceremony must be performed before felling one. Today, the New Zealand government, Māori communities, and conservation organizations are collaborating to preserve the kauri forests.

# Look to the kauri to support new beginnings.

Affirmation

Chapter 5

# SPIRIT: TREES OF THE LIMINAL SPACE

The element of Spirit (also referred to as ether or known to some as the soul) is within every living thing. Enter a wood or forest and you will sense the spirit of the place, the genius loci manifesting in the physical form of trees. In stories, trees move, speak, and house magical beings. Trees occupy the liminal space between the above and the below, the heavens and the Underworld—they are a bridge between the physical world and the spiritual world. In trees of the liminal space, we find those of the dawn and dusk, elves, spirits, trees of the underworlds, and rites to aid the passing of the dead.

# DATE PALM
*Phoenix dactylifera*

## *A rich source of sustenance, both physical and spiritual*

Thought to be the oldest cultivated plant in the world, the date palm is a flowering palm that produces the sweet fruit for which it is named. Originally grown in ancient Egypt and Mesopotamia, an area also known as the northern Fertile Crescent, historically between the Euphrates and Tigris Rivers, the date palm is now grown in North and East Africa, across the Middle East, South Asia, China, and the southwestern United States.

The botanical name for the date palm, *Phoenix dactylifera*, arose for two reasons. The genus name *Phoenix* comes from the tree's habit of releasing pollen in the early light of dawn. The clouds of pollen are reminiscent of smoke from a fire, from which the legendary golden phoenix may rise. The species part of the name, *dactylifera*, comes from *dactylos*, the Greek for "finger," and *fero*, Latin for "to bear," making the date palm a phoenix-birthing, finger-bearing tree.

If left to its own devices, the date palm can reach a height of over 100 feet (30 m) and live for a hundred years. Some argue that this tree is, in fact, a shrub, but its woody stems are wide and trunk-like, so many class it as a tree. As the tree grows, it drops its large fronds, leaving the old beginnings of these leaves behind and creating a textured trunk a little like the skin of a pineapple. The huge leaves can grow to 20 feet (6 m), and there are around 150 pinnate leaflets per stem. The leaves grow upward from the top of the trunk, creating an inside-out, umbrellalike effect. The fruits hang from the canopy in clusters of golden yellow to deep brown, ready-to-eat dates.

The date palm is most famous for being a rich source of food for desert dwellers and has sometimes been given the name Bread of the Sahara or Bread of the Desert. It is likely that this name is referring to the Thoory (Thuri) date variety, which grows near the Sahara

## SPIRIT CORRESPONDENCE

Dusk and Dawn • Spirituality • Fasting

border. This date has a thick skin and a pastry-like texture.

Date palms are either male or female (dioecious) and rely on wind pollination. When they are cultivated and farmed, commercial orchards will often hand-pollinate them to allow for a greater number of fruit-bearing female trees to be planted. Hand-pollination is carried out by climbing the tree and brushing the pollen across the tree's flowers. From the ground, the large bunches of tiny flowers look like bundles of wheat or barley. Some orchards use wind machines to speed up the process.

When dried, the fruit of the date palm is almost 70 percent sugar and is a favorite in both sweet and savory dishes around the world. Dates can be eaten fresh or dried, pitted and stuffed, and made into a honey-like syrup, a powder for flavoring, and even a liqueur known as Thibarine in Tunisia. The dried fruit can be ground into a powder to be used in bread when arable crops are in short supply, while the seeds can be ground into a coffee, which should be drunk with milk to avoid a sugar rush. Fully grown leaves can be made into mats, screens, baskets, and fans, and the soft wood of the trunk was once useful for building fences and rafts.

The date plays a part in several religions. In Judaism, Deborah, a Hebrew prophetess, sat under the date palm to pass judgments, and in this way the palm became a symbol of justice and righteousness. In ancient Egyptian mythology, an orchard of date palms greeted the dead in the Field of Reeds. In some versions of the story, the sky goddess Nut hands those entering the world of the dead the water of life, while the mother sky goddess Hathor hands them dates. In other versions, it is Nut's daughter Nephthys who offers both dates and water.

*In Judaism, Deborah, a Hebrew prophetess, sat under the date palm to pass judgments, and in this way the palm became a symbol of justice and righteousness.*

In Christianity, the leaves of the tree are an integral part of Palm Sunday. Palm Sunday celebrates the arrival of Jesus in Jerusalem after he spent forty days in the desert. The Bible tells of how Jesus spent time in the desert, praying and fasting before riding a donkey into the city of Jerusalem, where he was later tried and crucified. On the day he rode into the city, people laid palm leaves on the ground to pave his way. Palm leaves and small crosses made of them are still handed out in churches on Palm Sunday, and some keep them for Ash Wednesday the following year.

Ash Wednesday marks the start of Lent—a fast of forty days and forty nights leading up to Easter—and represents the time that Jesus spent in the desert. The palm leaves and crosses from the past year's Palm Sunday are burned, and the ash is used to mark the forehead of those who are about to begin Lent.

In Islam, it is said that Allah had some leftover clay when he had finished making Adam, and so he made the date palm. This tree is considered to be Allah's most precious gift. The date palm is also connected with fasting in the Muslim faith. Ramadan is a month when those following Islam do not eat or drink during daylight hours and take time to remember when the holy book known as the Quran was given to the Prophet Muhammad. During this time, it is traditional to break the fast in the evenings with dates, yogurt, and milk in a meal known as Iftar.

> Look to the date palm for sustenance in the desert.
>
> Affirmation

# ELM
*Ulmus*

## *A tree of spiritual significance connecting the earthly realm and other worlds*

The English elm (*Ulmus procera*) is native to Western and Southern Europe. There are around twenty species of elm, although there is often some dispute as to which belong to the *Ulmus* genus. Elms in Britain are associated with the ancient Romans, since they are often credited with bringing the elm to those shores. However, there were undoubtedly species of elm already growing in Britain at the time.

The ancient Romans used English elms to support vines for viticulture (grape production). In Book XVII, Chapter 15 of Pliny the Elder's *Naturalis Historia*, the Roman naturalist explains how to grow elms. He notes that the seeds should be collected in early spring, sown in fine soil, watered, cared for, and, when the trees are five years old, they can be transported to vineyards to support the growing vines.

*Ulmus procera* is a deciduous tree with serrated, asymmetrical leaves that turn golden in the fall. The branches grow close to the trunk base, giving the tree a dense, rounded canopy that is easily identifiable in the landscape. Elm flowers grow in dark pink and purple tassels that eventually transform into bunches of green samaras (winged seeds). The leaves have long been used as cattle food, and the trees are notably tolerant of pollution in cities.

The wood's resistance to water and rot made it an excellent material for water pipes, waterwheels, cartwheels, and barges during preindustrial times. Centuries earlier, the Greeks used the wood for temple doors and lintels, and when found more abundantly, elm was also a popular wood for coffins. Elm has been used medicinally by both Indigenous North Americans and Europeans, with remedies including treatments for coughs, colds, stomach complaints, and burns.

The Greeks often planted elm trees in graveyards, and the first-century Roman poet Virgil suggested that the elm was

# SPIRIT CORRESPONDENCE
## Sleep • Elves • Underworlds

connected with the Underworld as well as acting as a metaphysical crossroads for the human and fairy worlds. In Scandinavia, an elm in a farmyard can act as a Vårdträd, a supernatural gate between this world and the world of nature spirits. To add to the elm's ethereal reputation, the parasitic plant, common toothwort (*Lathraea squamaria*), will sometimes grow from the roots, its thin, papery buds looking moon-white against the bark.

The wych elm (*Ulmus glabra*) is most likely to be associated with elves and fairies and is native to Europe and Siberia. This species has slightly larger leaves and notched samara. The leaves are easily confused with hazel leaves, which explains this elm's other name, wych hazel. The tree, also known as the elven tree, is said to house elves who guard the souls of the dead and ensure their safe passage to the Underworld.

Carrying a piece of this tree in your pocket is said to repel witches. Indeed, in Oxfordshire, England, it was thought you could lift a witch's curse if you were struck nine times with a branch of wych elm. The name wych is more likely to have come from the Old English word *wice*, which means "weak" or "pliable," in reference to the wood's malleable nature. This pliability meant it was favored by Welsh archers for their longbows, as opposed to the English yew (*Taxus baccata*, see page 142), which was the more usual choice in Britain at the time.

The fact that the elm can drop dead branches with little warning, and at great risk to anyone below, further connects this tree with death and the Underworld. In Greek mythology, an elm grove sprang from the grieving tears and music of Orpheus when he lost his love Eurydice to the Underworld. Later, the tree became connected with the god of sleep, Morpheus, leading to the belief that anyone who slept beneath it would have nightmares.

Large elms were often used as markers in the landscape, providing valuable meeting places. One such elm species, *Ulmus americana*, survived the 1995 Oklahoma City terrorist bombing. In the months following this event, the tree provided the only shade in the parking lot in which it grew—it now stands as a symbol of hope.

Sadly, many elms across Europe and America have been destroyed by

Dutch elm disease, caused by the fungus *Ophiostoma novo-ulmi*, which was first identified in the Netherlands but did not necessarily originate there. The 1970s epidemic of the disease killed around twenty-five million trees in Britain alone. The fungal spores are spread by the elm bark beetle (the European species of which is *Scolytus multistriatus* and the North American, *Hylurgopinus rufipes*), which burrows into the bark, carrying the fungi with it. The beetles prefer older trees; hence, you will often find young saplings, while older specimens are now rare.

In Brighton, on England's south coast, there were once two elm trees known as the Preston Twins, both thought to be around four hundred years old. To protect these elms and other trees in the city, residents cut trenches between the trees to stop the fungus from spreading via the roots. They also removed infected branches to try to prevent the spread through the tree and set traps for the elm bark beetle. In 1998, the city was awarded the title of "Holder of the National Elm Collection" by the National Council for the Conservation of Plants and Gardens. Unfortunately, one of the twins succumbed to Dutch elm disease in 2019, but its sibling still stands.

In 2008, a cutting from one of the Preston Twins was sent to Amsterdam, Netherlands, a city that has also worked hard to combat the disease, inoculating young trees in the spring and breeding fungus-resistant elms. Amsterdam holds 75,000 specimens that grow along the edges of the city's canals and streets.

## Look to the elm for a bridge through the unknown.

Affirmation

# PALO SANTO
*Bursera graveolens*

## *A holy tree that calls for respect and restraint*

Palo santo has risen to fame thanks to its aromatic wood, used in shamanic, yogic, and holistic therapies. Its home is South America, and the name can be translated from Spanish as "sacred wood," "wood of saints," or "holy wood." Palo santo grows in the Yucatán Peninsula, southeast Mexico, Peru, and Venezuela, and is in the same family, Burseraceae, as frankincense (*Boswellia*, see page 26) and myrrh (*Commiphora erythraea*, see page 146).

Many palo santo trees are relatively short-lived, surviving only for around seventy years, but Indigenous people living on the land have reported that they can live for up to two hundred years. The tree can grow to approximately 60 feet (18 m) and is dioecious. In groves, there is often a group of female trees growing together with just one male.

The tree has smooth bark, and the wood inside is either yellow if it is a female tree, or a paler, yellowy-white wood that is lighter in weight if it is male. The leaves grow along the stems of the tree as even pairs of leaflets with serrated edges and a terminating leaf. The little white, bell-shaped flowers, which hang down between the leaves, have four petals. The fruits are small, round, and green to red, but it is the wood of the trunk that is most sought after.

A tea made from palo santo bark can be used for stomachaches and digestive complaints, and a liniment can also be applied for rheumatism. There is little scientific evidence as to why these remedies work, but it is perhaps the limonene within the bark that holds the key. It has been found that limonene is an antifungal and antiseptic oil; it may provide a medicinal use within the plant.

When palo santo wood is burned, the smoke can be used for ritual

## SPIRIT CORRESPONDENCE
Meditation • Serenity • Spirit World

purification, which clears a space of negative energy. The use of palo santo for smoke cleansing originates in the Incan tradition in South America. The descendants of the Incas in modern-day Peru are known as Q'ero people, and Q'ero shamans, known as curanderos, burn palo santo and use the smoke to clear sacred spaces. The smoke is also used to open a circle of protection around a ritual in order to remove negative energy, thoughts, and spirits, and to protect those within the circle.

The Q'ero are animists who believe that all life is sacred. Trees, including the palo santo, are seen as joining all life together: that of the heavens, the Earth, and the Underworld. This belief is represented in the ancient Chacana, also known as the Andean cross, a motif that symbolizes a bridge. The word *Chacana* means "to cross over," and while its meaning has never been fully understood, it could perhaps represent the liminal space between life and death and the cycle of life.

The limonene and terpenes (a compound produced by many plants and conifers) in palo santo resin is what gives the tree its unique character.

The combination of citrus and mint aromas has a soothing and meditative effect if used in aromatherapy. The relaxing effect is most likely due to the terpenes, and the limonene is uplifting. Together, they make a perfect combination for stress relief, relaxation, and meditation.

This combination of aromas is the reason behind the palo santo tree's success and may well put it at risk. This is because palo santo wood only releases its oils and scent once it has been decomposing in its natural environment for two to four years. The tree therefore needs to be felled, or to have fallen naturally, before it can start this process and become a commercially viable product. This has

*According to Incan folklore, a strong-willed spirit lives in the tree long after it has fallen, and this spirit must be treated with respect.*

led to deforestation and ultimately a depletion of palo santo forests.

According to Incan folklore, a strong-willed spirit lives in the tree long after it has fallen, and this spirit must be treated with respect. Very little is written about the legend, but perhaps this piece of folklore was a way of allowing the tree to rest for the four years necessary before it released its oils and could be used in sacred ceremonies.

The ability of palo santo smoke to clear negative spaces has given rise to the belief that the tree is one of protection, along with the claim that it can ward off evil spirits and has mystical powers. This is perhaps a reference to the limonene and terpenes within the wood, which might not have been identified by ancient cultures as medicinal, although the properties of the wood would have been observed.

In 2006, the Peruvian government listed the palo santo as critically endangered and banned live trees from being felled, allowing only the collection of naturally fallen wood for commercial use. Now, the palo santo has been removed from the list, thanks to communities advocating for its conservation. The Palo Santo Reforestation Program is one such organization and is working to restore the forests of Manabí in Ecuador. In 2020, the group reforested the region with four thousand native trees, many of which were the palo santo.

> **Look to the palo santo tree for patience when harvesting your rewards.**
>
> Affirmation

# YEW
*Taxus baccata*

## *A poisonous tree linked to graveyards, death, and the afterlife*

There are examples of the common yew (*Taxus baccata*) growing in Britain that are said to be the oldest living things in the world. However, botanists will tell you that aging a yew is difficult due to the way the trees grow. Yew trees can not only continue to thrive long after the original trunk has rotted away but also live through a fungal attack on the heartwood. This attack leaves the trunk hollow, making dendrochronology (a process of taking a section of the trunk and counting the rings of a tree to work out how old it is) impossible, as only the most recent rings remain.

Like most conifers, yew has small, straight, needle-shaped leaves. However, it does not produce cones. Instead, yew trees produce a bright red, berrylike aril that holds a seed inside. Yews are male or female (dioecious), with the male trees producing clusters of tiny, creamy white flowers that release pollen. The flowers of the female tree are small buds that eventually develop into the bright red arils. Despite being toxic, the seeds within the aril are spread with the help of birds, such as migrating waxwings (*Bombycilla garrulus*), which gorge themselves on vast quantities and, due to the tree's toxicity, vomit up the seeds away from the tree, inadvertently giving the seeds a new place to take root and grow.

Yew is famous for its use in the making of longbows throughout the medieval period. There is even evidence to suggest that hunting bows were made from yew as far back as the Neolithic Period, leading to its nickname the "bow tree." This may also come from its Latin name, as the genus *Taxus* comes from the Greek work *toxon*, which means "bow." This word would later become toxin, used as a catch-all for all poisons.

Longbows were a crucial part of British culture for most of the medieval period. This was cemented in 1349,

## SPIRIT CORRESPONDENCE
### Graveyards • Ghosts • Battlefields

when Edward III proclaimed that every able-bodied man must learn archery, and then again almost two hundred years later, when Henry VIII decreed that all men must practice with a longbow daily and have a bow and arrow at the ready at home. Yews were a handy source of wood for bows in times of war, and at one point exporting yew from Britain was banned.

Throughout history, the yew tree has been inextricably linked with death and rebirth. Indeed, sleeping under a yew was said to court death. Its leaves, bark, and seeds are highly toxic, and yew trees are often found growing in graveyards or on ancient burial mounds. The Greeks and Romans believed the yew to be a funerary tree and often planted it on tombs and at the gates of graveyards. In Celtic mythology, the yew tree is

> *In Celtic mythology, the yew tree is connected with the Underworld, death, and eternal life.*

connected with the Underworld, death, and eternal life. It is also associated with the festival of Samhain (a Celtic festival celebrated at a similar time to Halloween), a night when both the dead and the living can walk together.

The presence of yew trees in graveyards has been a subject of much debate. It's been argued that the yew tree was at first a meeting place for the community. The church was built beside the yew tree in the hope that the pagans gathering underneath would come into the church and be reformed. Another theory is that yew trees were valued as a resource but poisonous to cattle, so they were planted beside churches and in graveyards since cattle were not allowed to graze there.

Whether it was the church or the yew that came first is a question that will perhaps never be definitively answered. However, it is irrefutable that the yew and death are close friends, with the roots of the trees often growing through old graves and becoming entwined with those interred below.

The yew tree's association with rebirth lies in stark contrast to the plethora of lore connecting the tree with death. Perhaps this is because it was observed that if a yew tree dropped a branch, new roots would shoot from it, but it could also have to do with the estimated age of some yew trees—Britain is said to be home to some of the world's oldest specimens, the majority of which can be found in churchyards.

One such yew is the Fortingall Yew, which grows in the graveyard of Fortingall church in Perthshire, Scotland. It was Daines Barrington, an English lawyer, antiquary, and naturalist, who in 1769 first measured and noted the 52-foot (16 m) circumference of the tree's trunk. The trunk later split, and a funeral procession could fit between the two parts in order to walk the body beneath the arch of the tree, thus guiding the Christian spirit to the afterlife. Soon, the tree became a ring of trunks, and in the 1800s, railings and a stone wall were placed around the tree to protect it from Victorian souvenir hunters.

Lining the path to the entrance of the sixth-century church at Nevern in Pembrokeshire, Wales, are yew trees that have become known as the Bleeding Yews. Perhaps seven hundred years old, they drip a red, sap-like substance reminiscent of blood. Legend has it that this is in sympathy with the crucifixion of Jesus. Another tale tells of how one of the yews weeps for a monk who was hanged for a crime he did not commit.

Elsewhere in Wales, an Ystradgynlais church has four yews that are kept neatly trimmed, for legend here tells that when the smallest yew reaches the height of the bell tower, the world will come to an end.

## Look to the yew for ancient roots.

Affirmation

# MYRRH
*Commiphora erythraea*

## *A resinous tree of spiritual and religious importance*

The myrrh tree and its resin have been part of human culture since the Neolithic period. Until the second century BCE, myrrh was only found in the historical region of South Arabia (now the Arabian Peninsula). The domestication of camels during this time meant myrrh could finally be transported to the ports on the peninsula's coast and from there distributed around the world.

Like frankincense (see page 26), its aromatic resin was the prize—milky sap is collected from gashes in the tree and dried to form a resin for use as incense. In the second century BCE, 2¼ pounds (1 kg) of myrrh resin cost the equivalent of a month's wages for poorer people.

A thorny tree in the Burseraceae family, myrrh can grow in the harshest of conditions, among the rocky hills of the Arabian landscape, and can reach a height of 10 feet (3 m). The bark cracks with age and releases the resin, which hardens and can be collected without having to slash the bark. The tree will often become gnarled, with the boughs forming a canopy that flattens out at the top. Small, oval leaves grow among the thorns, with one main leaf and two leaflets just below on each side. Tiny, yellow flowers emerge from the base of the leaves and develop into small, green fruits.

Pharaoh Hatshepsut ruled as queen regent between 1479 BCE and 1458 BCE and is considered ancient Egypt's most formidable female ruler. On an expedition to Punt, Hatshepsut's delegation is said to have brought back around thirty myrrh trees for the queen as well as huge amounts of myrrh resin. It is said that one of the myrrh trees was planted next to a mortuary temple called Djeser-Djeseru, a vast sandstone building with terraces carved into the cliffs at Deir el-Bahari in western Thebes. The temple also once held

# SPIRIT CORRESPONDENCE
## Mysteries • Anointing • Blessings

carvings displaying Hatshepsut's trade with Punt. If you visit the temple today, you will see a tree stump and a sign stating that it is the remains of one of the myrrh trees brought back from the Punt expedition.

Myrrh resin is largely used as incense and perfume in spiritual and holy rites. This practice dates back to ancient Egypt, when myrrh oil was used in mummification to anoint the dead, reduce decay, deodorize, and disinfect. It was known that myrrh had preservative qualities, as well as antibacterial and antifungal properties, and it was effective for mummification when used with other ingredients like beeswax, conifer resin, and gum arabic. Myrrh

*The story of the Queen of Sheba tells how she brought gifts of frankincense, myrrh, gold, and jewels when she visited King Solomon.*

also played a part in ancient Egyptian rituals for worshipping the sun god Ra, in which an unspecified gold resin was burned at dawn, myrrh at noon, and frankincense at sunset. Greek soldiers were also aware of myrrh's antibacterial properties, often carrying it into battle to treat wounds.

Many cultures have used myrrh as an anointing oil, and myrrh is significant in various religions. It is often associated with deities, including Isis, Egyptian goddess of the sky. When her brother Osiris was killed by their brother Set, she put the pieces of his body back together, subsequently becoming associated with death and resurrection and, in turn, myrrh.

In Greek mythology, the goddess Aphrodite became jealous of the mortal Myrrha's beauty and cursed her to fall in love with her own father. Unwittingly, Myrrha's father lay with her and she became pregnant, resulting in the birth of the god Adonis. When her father found out who Adonis was, he threatened to kill Myrrha. She called to the gods for protection, and Aphrodite took pity on her and turned her into the myrrh tree.

In Jewish, Christian, and Muslim texts, the story of the Queen of Sheba tells how she brought gifts of frankincense, myrrh, gold, and jewels when she visited King Solomon. The work of Flavius Josephus, a first-century Jewish priest and historian, describes how the Queen of Sheba's myrrh trees were housed in the gardens of Jericho. Myrrh is also mentioned in the Muslim Quran as a healing tree and used as an offering in the Hindu faith during *puja* ceremonies, which honor one or more Hindu gods.

Myrrh also appears in the religious ceremonies of Orthodox Christians, Catholics, and Lutherans. It was one of the first gifts brought by the Magi on the birth of Jesus, who was anointed with myrrh when he died. In the Book of Exodus, God gives Moses instructions on Mount Sinai for using myrrh to make an anointing oil. God then tells Moses to explain this to the Israelites, saying: "This will be My sacred anointing oil for the generations to come."

In the Greek Orthodox Church, the sacred anointing oil is known as chrism, myrrh, or myron. This oil is prepared once every ten years and consecrated by the Ecumenical Patriarch of Constantinople (now Istanbul). Much mystery surrounds the ingredients of chrism, and while it usually has a base of olive oil, within the Greek Orthodox Church's recipe there are a further fifty-seven ingredients, one of which may well be myrrh.

The process of creating the chrism starts on Holy Monday (the day after Palm Sunday) and it is consecrated on Holy Thursday. Chrism is used in baptisms. Once you are anointed with the oil, you become a Christian, a process first described by the fourth-century Cyril of Jerusalem. He described how the oil would be used to anoint a person's forehead, ears, nostrils, and breast. Chrism is also used in the Catholic confirmation ceremony.

## Look to myrrh for initiation.

Affirmation

# INDIAN BANYAN
*Ficus bengalensis*

## *A protective tree offering physical and spiritual sanctuary*

The banyan tree is renowned for its record-breaking size—it can spread over an area of up to almost 62,300 feet (19,000 m). In the Hindu religion the banyan is regarded as the world tree under which, much like the pipal tree (*Ficus religiosa,* see page 90), you can find enlightenment and wisdom.

The banyan is the Tree of Knowledge and the cosmic spirit that supports the universe, connecting the Earth with the heavens. For all these reasons, it is also known as the Tree of Life. Native to the Indian subcontinent, it is India's national tree, and beneath many you will find temples and community meeting places.

The banyan tree's leaves are oval, thick, green, and leathery, and about the size of an adult hand. The fruits are small, red, and fig-like. As with many trees in the fig family, Moraceae, the flowers are found within the fruits and pollinated by the fig wasp (*Blastophaga psenes*). The seed begins its transformation as an epiphyte, deposited via the excrement of a bird or small mammal. It grows in the branches of another tree, initially taking nothing from its host tree but support while harvesting nutrients from the air. However, as the seed grows, it consumes the original tree by sending down aerial roots that develop into strong prop roots.

The tree creates multiple trunks, growing ever outward, until it is made of hundreds of trunks and thousands of aerial roots. The tree's ability to consume another tree led eighteenth- and nineteenth-century European explorers to call it the strangler fig.

Several banyan trees in India are significant because of their size. One stands in Kolkata in the botanical gardens and is thought to be 250 years old. The canopy is almost 500 feet (152 m) in diameter, and it is said to be able to shelter around two thousand

## SPIRIT CORRESPONDENCE
### Shapeshifters • Resurrection • Gathering Places

people. This tree draws hundreds of visitors every year and, due to its thousands of aerial roots, has earned the nickname *bahupada*, meaning "one with many feet." It has survived three cyclones, the most recent of which was in 2020, and at the heart of the tree, where the trunk has long since decayed, there stands a monument in memory of the tree's original trunk.

A second notable tree stands around 16 miles (25 km) from the city of Kadiri, in the state of Andhra Pradesh. Known as Thimmamma's Banyan Tree, it is thought to be five hundred years old. The canopy has a circumference of 2,776 feet (846 m), and the tree has more than four thousand aerial roots. So vast is the tree that a temple has been built inside, and visiting pilgrims remove their shoes before walking under the canopy of this sacred specimen. Each year, a folk festival takes place there with outdoor theater, music, and entertainment.

The tree holds the story of a woman named Thimmamma. When her husband died, she carried out the practice of sati, involving the widow joining her husband on the funeral pyre. The tree grows on the site where Thimmamma made her sacrifice, and legend tells that one of the pyre's supporting poles self-rooted—with its help, Thimmamma transformed herself into the banyan tree, becoming the goddess of the tree. She is said to bless those who wish to have children.

The banyan tree's place in the Hindu faith sees it linked to a Trimurti of gods, with the roots being the great creator himself, Brahma; the bark, Vishnu the protector; and the aerial roots, Shiva the destroyer. It is the home of the divine presence of these gods and is also associated with Yama, the god of death and justice. In the *Mahābhārata*, one of the texts revered in the Hindu religion as holding the faith's written traditions, a woman named Savitri loses her husband, Satyavan, and lays him under

*In the Philippines, the banyan is known as the balete tree, where demons, spirits, and lost souls dwell.*

a banyan. Impressed by her reverence for her husband, Yama offers to grant her a gift, barring restoring her husband's life. She asks for one thousand sons, and Yama realizes that for this to come to pass, he has no choice but to resurrect Satyavan. Her love for her husband, as well as her trickery and resolve, is celebrated each year when married Hindu women tie ribbons to the banyan tree during the festival of Vat Purnima. Through these stories, the banyan tree has become associated with fertility, life, and resurrection, and it is seen as a granter of wishes, wealth, and good luck.

As well as being a place of gathering for religious ceremony and community celebration, the banyan tree is said to be a home to magical beings. In the Philippines, the banyan is known as the balete tree, where demons, spirits, and lost souls dwell. Several folkloric beings are associated with the tree, some of which are malevolent, while others grant good fortune. The Aswang is a legendary flying, vampire-like creature that can shape-shift into a terrifying dog, cat, or pig. The Tikbalang was originally a nature spirit but gradually evolved, with the influence of colonists, into a bipedal creature with a horse's head and legs and a man's torso and arms. He is a trickster, able to transmute into different forms, and will lead you from the path if you're not careful.

More benign creatures of the banyan include the Diwata, a genius loci (spirit of a place) that lives in the tree and will protect the area in which it dwells. It takes the form of a fairy or nymphlike creature and possesses magical powers, which it may use to help you. The Kapre, on the other hand, is neither good nor evil, but simply an 8-foot-tall (2.4 m) tree-dweller who likes to stand beneath the banyan tree smoking cigars.

# Look to the banyan for shelter and comfort.

Affirmation

# HAWTHORN

*Crataegus monogyna*

*A magical tree with many names, favored by the fairy folk*

Such is the ancient significance of the hawthorn that in *Vickery's Folk Flora* you will find almost ninety colloquial names for this tree and its fruits in Britain and Ireland alone. Haw-bush, quick, and may-bush are the three most common: haw-bush on account of the berries, or haws, in late summer and early fall; quick due to the way the tree grows; and may-bush because the tree flowers in May. Hawthorn is one of the most common trees in folklore and inextricably linked with the fairy folk.

The hawthorn can grow to around 33 feet (10 m) and is one of the first trees to flower in spring—as such, it is a symbol of hope. The bright white, five-petaled flowers carry stamens composed of white filaments tipped by tiny, black anthers. The lobed leaves are mid-green and unfurl before the flowers, making it easy to distinguish from its cousin, the blackthorn (*Prunus spinosa*). Blackthorn typically flowers in mid-spring and then produces leaves, whereas hawthorn has leaves in mid-spring and flowers in late spring.

The thorns of the hawthorn are not as treacherous as the blackthorn's, and the red haws grow among them in early fall. *Haw* in Old English can be translated as "hedge," and it is from this word that we get the surnames Hayward and Haywood. The hayward was once responsible for maintaining the hedges and boundary of the village, even repatriating stray animals and cattle. Haywards carried a hawthorn staff to ward off adders (*Vipera berus*), Britain's only poisonous snake, and one that finds the lower stories of hawthorn hedges a good place to sunbathe.

The quickest way to grow a hedge is by using hazel and/or hawthorn, and this has been called a quick set hedge since the 1400s. However, quick does not refer to the speed of growth but the fact that the hedge is planted using

## SPIRIT CORRESPONDENCE
Fae Folk • Thresholds • Magic

live cuttings, meaning the saplings are already rooted and then cut, ready to shoot new branches. The leaves can be used to make a tea and the haws a jelly, fruit leather, ketchup, or tonic. The haws should not be eaten raw, as they may induce stomach upsets. Caution should also be used if you have a heart condition, as hawthorn berries can reduce blood pressure.

England's Glastonbury Thorn is one of the most famous hawthorn trees that stands alone and is revered as a magical tree. This hawthorn is a cultivar known as *Crataegus monogyna* 'Biflora', which flowers twice a year. The story goes that Joseph of Arimathea, the biblical figure who oversaw Jesus's burial, visited Wearyall Hill, where the hawthorn stands, and plunged his staff into the ground. From the staff grew the hawthorn. The tree that stands there today was planted in 1951, after the original was destroyed during the English Civil War in the mid-seventeenth century.

Hawthorns can be found beside clootie wells, a tradition hailing from Scotland but also practiced in many places in Britain. In this tradition, if you are unwell, a *cloot* (Scots for "rag")

is tied to a tree beside a sacred well or spring. As the rag rots away, the illness will leave you. This tradition is still practiced today, although sadly many forget to use biodegradable fabrics.

In many traditions, particularly in Ireland, the hawthorn is the tree of the fae folk and should only be cut with great caution. Any hawthorn standing alone should not be felled at all. Eddie Lenihan is a seanchaí/Irish folklorist who has collected hundreds of accounts of Irish folklore in the oral tradition. In his book *Meeting the Other Crowd*, there are multiple stories of hawthorns standing alone in a field, revered by the locals, until an overzealous or greedy landowner tries to fell the tree. Inevitably, grave misfortune befalls them—usually involving a family tragedy and the burning or loss of property—which is attributed to the wrath of the hawthorn fairies.

A modern example of the strength of this lore is the story of the Latoon Fairy Tree in County Clare, Ireland. This was reported in *The New York Post* in 2005 and in several local and national news publications in Ireland. The Latoon Fairy Tree stands on the bank of the

*It is said that if you wash your face on May 1 in early morning dew that has gathered on the hawthorn, it will give your skin everlasting youth.*

M18 motorway (freeway), in an area known locally as the Newmarket-on-Fergus bypass. The tree drew attention when it delayed the motorway's construction by almost ten years. Lenihan led the campaign to save the tree, stating that "death and great misfortune" would come to pass if it were cut down. The tree was, indeed, saved and stands there to this day.

Hawthorn is considered a charm of protection if hung above doorways to ward off unwanted visitors, such as fairies or those practicing dark magic. The ancient Romans used the hawthorn as a protective charm, placing a sprig of hawthorn in the cradles of newborns. However, if you bring flowering hawthorn into the house, you are back to the fairy-tree situation and bad luck will befall you. Perhaps this is because the flowers are said to smell like decomposing corpses as they rot, which was first recorded in 1627 by Francis Bacon. It's since been discovered that a chemical in the flowers called trimethylamine is identical to the one in rotting meat.

The hawthorn is mostly associated with May Day; hence, May flower as a colloquial name. It is said that if you wash your face on May 1 in early morning dew that has gathered on the hawthorn, it will give your skin everlasting youth. As with most plants, though, the flowering of the hawthorn does not always coincide with the first day in May, so if a servant could find one flowering on that day, they would be gifted a bowl of cream for their family.

## Look to the hawthorn as a source of magic.

Affirmation

# INDEX

## A
African mythology 29, 42–3
Anglo-Saxons 28, 72, 111
apple, wild (*Malus sylvestris*) 108–11
*Arabian Nights* 110
ash (*Fraxinus excelsior*) 48–51
Ash Wife 50
avocado (*Persea americana*) 30–3
Aztec mythology 32–3

## B
Bacon, Francis 157
baobab (*Adansonia digitata*) 40–3
Barrington, Daines 145
bats 57
bay laurel (*Laurus nobilis*) 74–7
Bible 10, 12, 28, 37, 103, 106, 133
birch (*Betula*) 18–21
Bleeding Yews 145
Bock, Hieronymus 70
Bonaparte, Napoleon 76
Buddhism 78, 90–3
butterflies 119

## C
Caribbean folklore 58–9
*Ceiba pentandra* 57–9
Celtic mythology 12, 46–7, 48, 73, 144
Chapman, John (Johnny Appleseed) 108–10
Charles I 51
Charles II 12–13, 122
cherry laurel (*Prunus laurocerasus*) 77
Chinese medicine 80–1
Christianity 12, 25, 72, 133, 149
cinchona (*Cinchona officinalis*) 120–3
coco de mer (*Lodoicea maldivica*) 60–3
crab apple 108–11

## D
date palm (*Phoenix dactylifera*) 130–3
Disocorides 46
Doctrine of Signatures 72
Druids 47, 73

## E
Edward III 144
Egypt, ancient 22, 26, 28, 54, 100, 102, 130, 147–8
Egyptian mythology 54, 132, 148
elm (*Ulmus*) 134–7

## F
fig (*Ficus carica*) 104–7
Fortingall Yew 145
frankincense (*Boswellia*) 26–9

## G
Gerard, John 106
ginkgo (*Ginkgo biloba*) 78–81
Glastonbury Thorn 156
golden wattle (*Acacia pycnantha*) 52–5
Graves, Robert 48
Greece, ancient 46, 60, 76, 134, 144, 148
Greek mythology 12, 14, 24–5, 47, 50, 66, 74, 102–3, 106, 110, 136, 148

## H
Hatshepsut 147–8
Hawai'i 117–19
hawthorn (*Crataegus monogyna*) 155–7
hazel (*Corylus*) 44–7
Henry VIII 12, 25, 144
Herodotus 54
Hinduism 90, 93, 149, 150–3
Hiroshima, Japan 81
honeycreepers 119
hornbill, silvery-cheeked 65

## I
Incense Route 26
Indian banyan (*Ficus bengalensis*) 150–3
Indigenous Australians 52, 55
Indigenous North Americans 16–17, 35–37, 44, 50, 55, 71–2, 82–5, 134
Indigenous South Americans 57–8, 120–2, 138–40
Irish mythology 18, 96–7, 156–7
Islam 103, 133, 149

## J
Jainism 90
Japanese mythology 114–15
Jesus 28, 103, 106, 133, 145, 149, 156
Josephus 149
Joshua tree (*Yucca brevifolia*) 35–7
Judaism 22–4, 132, 149
jumping the broom 20–1

## K

Kaempfer, Engelbert 80
kapok (*Ceiba pentandra*) 57-9
kauri pine (*Agathis australis*) 125-7
koa (*Acacia koa*) 117-19

## L

Laidley Worm of Spindleston Heugh 96
Latoon Fairy Tree 156-7
laurel wreaths 76
Lenihan, Eddie *The Other Crowd* 156-7
lightning 12, 16
Linnaeus, Carl 122
longbows 136, 142-4
Louis XIV of France 122

## M

magic guarri (*Euclea divinorum*) 65-7
malaria 120-3
Māori mythology 126-7
maple syrup 82-5
Muhammad, Prophet 103, 133
murrelet, marbled 16
myrrh (*Commiphora erythraea*) 147-9

## N

New Zealand 125-7
Noble, David 86-8
Norse mythology 12, 48-50, 96, 110-11

## O

oak (*Quercus*) 10-13
oak gall ink 10

Oak King 13
olive (*Olea europaea*) 100-3
Olympic Games 76
Ovid *Metamorphoses* 29

## P

palo santo (*Bursera graveolens*) 138-41
parrot, Seychelles black 63
Philippine mythology 153
phoenix 29, 130
pipal (*Ficus religiosa*) 90-3
Pliny the Elder 29, 133-4
pomegranate (*Punica granatum*) 22-5

## Q

Queen of Sheba 149
quinine 120-3

## R

redwood (*Sequoia*) 14-17
Rome, ancient 12, 22, 26, 29, 46, 76, 102, 107, 120, 134, 144, 157
rowan (*Sorbus aucuparia*) 95-7

## S

salmon, Coho 16
Saxon mythology 12
Seychelles 60-3
Shakespeare, William *Macbeth* 28-9
shield bugs 119
Shinto 78, 114-15
Sikhism 90
Slavic mythology 21, 73
Solomon 24, 149
Soren, David 120
sugar maple (*Acer saccharum*) 82-5

## T

Talbot, Robert 122
Taoism 78
Thoreau, Henry David 108
Tongue, Ruth 50
tree frogs 57

## U

UNESCO World Heritage Sites 63, 74, 92

## V

*Vickery's Folk Flora* 155
Virgil 134-6

## W

Wales, William and Catherine 63
wassailing 51, 111
waxwings 142
Welsh mythology 21
willow (*Salix*) 70-3
Wollemi pine (*Wollemia nobilis*) 86-9

## Y

yew (*Taxus baccata*) 142-5
Yoshino cherry (*Prunus x yedoensis*) 112-15

## Z

Zoroastrianism 22
Zulus 66

## ACKNOWLEDGMENTS

Writing and researching this book has taken me on a journey across the world to explore Indigenous cultures, hidden traditions, and, ultimately, the relationship humans have had with trees for millions of years. It is the people who walked the Earth before me and kept the stories and lore of the trees with them as they went, passing them down from generation to generation until eventually they appeared here in the pages of this book, whom I must thank for the knowledge and wisdom held here.

Thanks also go to my family and friends for their support when I holed myself away in the study for hours at a time, emerging only for school runs, to cook dinners, and to share random and arcane facts about trees in a most unsolicited manner, yet one that they bore with grace and even interest.

The team at Quarto has been an absolute pleasure to work with, from Jo Lightfoot and her work on the inception of this book to the team who worked hard to bring the book to life: Emma Harverson, Ella Whiting, Caroline West, and Martina Calvio, and the stunning illustrations created by Julia Asenbaum.

The trees deserve a mention, too, for without them there would be no book, quite literally in the case of the paper that holds the words I crafted. Finally, dear reader, thank you for sharing this journey with me, and I hope you enjoyed reading this book as much as I did writing it. From root to bough, trees truly do hold the wisdom, magic, and life upon which we depend as humans.

### ABOUT THE AUTHOR

Dawn Nelson is an author, consultant, reenactor, folklorist, performance storyteller, and all-round word-witch specializing in landscape, nature, and heritage interpretation. She lives within the beautiful South Downs National Park in South East England and regularly works with heritage sites, museums, schools, and outdoor educators to bring landscape, heritage, and nature to life for all through stories and folklore. Her belief is that in order to connect with our inner selves and the rhythms of nature that lie deep within us, we must first reconnect with the natural world that surrounds us and the stories it holds to rewild ourselves through story. You can keep up-to-date with Dawn's work by visiting her website www.thebarddawn.co.uk and finding her on socials @thebarddawn.